SPARTA

SPARTA

A. H. M. JONES, LL.D., D.D.

PROFESSOR OF ANCIENT HISTORY
IN THE UNIVERSITY OF CAMBRIDGE

HARVARD UNIVERSITY PRESS
CAMBRIDGE, MASSACHUSETTS
1967

First printed in 1967

PRINTED IN GREAT BRITAIN

PREFACE

I WAS impelled to write this book by having to prepare a course of lectures on Sparta as a special subject in the Cambridge Classical Tripos for 1965–6. I wrote it in Egypt in the winter of 1964–5, making use of the rather limited resources of the Classical Library at Giza University—which may account for, if not excuse, some of its errors, omissions and incoherencies. Professor Andrewes, of New College, Oxford, read it in manuscript, and Mr. Geoffrey de Ste. Croix, of the same College, in galley proof. Both disapproved of it heartily, and I am therefore all the more grateful to them for their kindness in correcting many errors and supplying many omissions.

Owing to illness the book has spent a long time in proof, and I am grateful to Sir Basil Blackwell for being patient with my delays.

A. H. M. JONES

Jesus College, Cambridge
August, 1966

v

CONTENTS

MAPS

viii

FOLK MEMORY

THE Spartans had short memories. When Herodotus visited Sparta, perhaps about the middle of the fifth century, he was able to pick up a good many stories about Cleomenes, the king of the Agiad line who had reigned just before the battle of Marathon in 490. Not that all Herodotus' information about Cleomenes came from Spartan sources; he drew much from the traditions of Argos, Corinth and Athens. But there are a number of anecdotes which clearly derive from the descendants of Cleomenes' half-brothers, Leonidas and Cleombrotus, and one clearly came ultimately from Gorgo, his daughter, who married Leonidas.[1] Herodotus' picture of Cleomenes is, however, greatly distorted; on a simple point of fact he says that his reign was short,[2] while from the information that he gives us it appears that he must have ruled for nearly thirty years. Herodotus learned something about Demaratus, the king of the other (Eurypontid) line contemporary with Cleomenes, but this he probably got from Demaratus' descendants, who ruled a petty principality in the Troad under Persian suzerainty; most of his information is about Demaratus' deposition through the intrigues of Cleomenes. He also knew about the family affairs of Cleomenes' father, Anaxandridas, and Demaratus' father, Ariston, which bore on the succession in both dynasties. They were, he said, contemporary with Croesus, king of Lydia (560–546), and he was told a slightly fabulous story of the defeat of Tegea in their joint reign. Of Leon and Agasicles, the grandfathers of Cleomenes and Demaratus, he knew nothing except that they were successful in all their wars except against Tegea. He was told of a yet earlier and

[1] Herod. V. 51.　　　　[2] Herod. V. 48.

unsuccessful war against Tegea; no kings are named, and the story probably comes from a Tegeate source.

Except for a Messenian war Herodotus records nothing earlier than this. The earlier history was not perhaps relevant to his theme, but he would probably have worked in anything of interest. Later historians knew of two Messenian wars, the first conquest of Messenia under King Theopompus, who was nine generations (inclusive) back from Demaratus, and the reduction of the revolt of the Messenians two generations later. But this information came not from oral tradition or historical records, but from the poems of Tyrtaeus, who wrote during and after the second Messenian war. We possess the lines which give the information, and it is plain that there was no other evidence. 'To our godbeloved King Theopompus, through whom we conquered spacious Messene'; and 'About it they fought nineteen years ceaselessly, ever keeping up a patient spirit, the spearmen, our fathers' fathers. But in the twentieth year they left the fat fields and fled from the mighty Ithomian mountains.'[1] Tyrtaeus did not mention the kings who reigned in his time, and later historians supplied their names by counting the generations.[2] There are some anecdotes about Theopompus and his contemporary king Polydorus, but their value is dubious—except in so far as they may derive from Tyrtaeus.

The genealogies of the two royal houses and the succession of the two lines of kings are the one thing that tradition might have been expected to preserve. Herodotus[3] gives the full genealogy of Leonidas, the Agiad king who fell at Thermopylae in 480 and of Leotychidas the Eurypontid king who won the battle of Mycale in 479. They both go back to Heracles, but it is obviously foolish to expect a true record from the earliest period. The Agiad line agrees with the accounts given by the later historians, and preserved for us by Pausanias, who wrote a Baedeker of Greece in the second century A.D. This is on the assumption that in every case son succeeded father. But in the

---

[1] *Anth. Lyr. Gr.*[3], fr. 4.   [2] Paus. IV. xv. 2–3.   [3] VII. 204, VIII. 131.

2

Eurypontid line Herodotus' genealogy is completely at variance with Pausanias' list. Herodotus says that the ancestry of Leotychidas, who was of a collateral branch, intruded on Demaratus' deposition, was Theopompus, Anaxandridas, Archidamus, Anaxilaus, Leotychidas, Hippocratidas, Agesilaus (or Agis), Menares, of whom all except the last two were kings of Sparta. This implies that Agesilaus (Agis), Leotychidas' grandfather, was a younger brother of Agasicles, Demaratus' grandfather. But Pausanias[1] gives the succession of kings as Theopompus, his grandson Zeuxidamus (his son Archidamus having predeceased him), and then, son after father, Anaxidamus, Archidamus, Agasicles, Ariston.[a]

What makes matters worse, Rhianus, a learned poet of the third century B.C., made Leotychidas (in Herodotus' line of descent) king at the time of the second Messenian war,[2] and Plutarch[3] in the second century A.D. mentions a King Leotychidas I, and a commentator on Alcman[4] of the same period states that the king alluded to by that poet, whose date is very uncertain, but long before Leotychidas, the victor of Mycale, was Leotychidas. There is no reliable information (and practically no information at all) about any Spartan king of either line between Theopompus (and perhaps his contemporary Polydorus) and Leon and Agasicles who reigned seven generations later. The Spartans did not even know who the kings of the Eurypontid house were.

Later Greek chronologists gave precise dates for the two Messenian wars, and for the Spartan kings from the return of the Heraclids (what we call the Dorian invasion). Some of these are preserved by Pausanias;[5] the first Messenian war was from 743 to 724 and the second from 685 to 668. Eusebius, the great Christian historian of Constantine's reign, put the earlier reigns from the return of the Heraclids to Theopompus and Polydorus into his Chronicle of World History.[6] Theopompus is dated 785–738

---

[1] III. vii. 5–6.   [2] Paus. IV. xv. 2.   [3] *Mor.* 224cd, *Lyc.* 13.   [4] *P. Oxy.* 2390.
[5] IV. v. 10, xiii. 7, xv. 1, xxiii. 4.   [6] Eus. *Chron.* I. 222–5, ed. Schoene.

3

and Polydorus 758–753. These two sets of dates come from slightly variant chronological schemes, those of Sosibius the Laconian and of Apollodorus of Athens;[b] for on the evidence of Tyrtaeus Theopompus lived to complete the conquest of Messenia. All these dates are, however, it is generally admitted, based on counts of generations, and the generations are all much longer than in any historical dynasties. Modern scholars have argued that a clue to the date of the first Messenian war is to be found in the list of Olympic victors, which is probably mainly genuine. There was a run of Messenian athletes who won the foot race, which ends with Leochares in 736. The first Spartan victor was Acanthus in 720.[1] This perhaps proves that the Messenian state existed as late as 736 (though the presidents of the games may have recognized exiles), but Messenian athletes may not have been so successful in the last decades of Messenian independence.

In the fifth and fourth centuries B.C. a different chronology was current. Epaminondas when he refounded Messene in 369 declared that the city had been destroyed 230 years before.[2] This puts the end of the second Messenian war in 600 and the first Messenian war therefore about 690–670. Aristotle found no difficulty in dating Lycurgus, whom he believed to be the uncle of Charilaus, ten generations before Demaratus, to 776 B.C.[3] Thucydides[4] believed that the reforms attributed by Herodotus to Lycurgus took place something over 400 years before the end of the Peloponnesian war in 404 B.C.

[1] Eus. *Chron.* I, 195, ed. Schoene.   [2] Plut. *Mor.* 194b, Aelian, *Var. Hist.* XIII. 42.
[3] Plut. *Lyc.* 1, Arist. *Pol.* II. x. 2, 1271b.   [4] I. 18.

4

LYCURGUS

FROM the fifth century B.C. Lycurgus was worshipped at Sparta as the great lawgiver who had in the dim past laid down the Spartan constitution and social and military system, just as it existed in historical times (whenever the author wrote). He did not figure in either royal genealogy. According to Herodotus[1] he was regent for his nephew Leobotes, six generations before Polydorus in the Agiad dynasty (Apollodoran date 1025–988).

The unwary reader of Herodotus might, however, but for the precise dating to Leobotes, have inferred that Lycurgus was a much more recent figure. Herodotus begins by saying that 'in the reigns of Leon and Hegesicles in Sparta the Lacedaemonians were successful in their other wars, but failed against Tegea only. And still earlier than that they were almost the most badly governed of all the Hellenes, and had the worst relations with their neighbours. They changed to good government in this way.' He then tells the story of Lycurgus and his reforms, and resumes: 'after this change they were well governed . . . and, seeing that they lived in a good country and had a large population, immediately shot up and flourished. And they were no longer content to keep the peace, but despising the Arcadians and thinking themselves stronger they consulted the oracle at Delphi.' He then goes on to describe the disastrous attack on Tegea and next its final conquest under Anaxandridas and Ariston.

No reader could guess that ten or eleven generations had intervened between the reforms of Lycurgus and the unsuccessful attack on Tegea and its ultimate reduction. Herodotus' informants

[1] I. 65.

would seem to have been talking about the Tegeate wars a generation or two before Anaxandridas and Ariston, and by implication to have dated Lycurgus to that period, though they specifically equated him with Leobotes.

According to Herodotus' elder contemporary, the poet Simonides,[1] he was the younger son of Prytanis, five generations before Theopompus in the Eurypontid line (Apollodoran date 978–929), brother of Eunomus and regent for his nephew. Later authors[2] accepted a slight variant of this, that he was the uncle and guardian of Charilaus, two generations before Theopompus in the Eurypontid line (Apollodoran date 884–824). Aristotle[3] accepted this version, but dated Lycurgus about 776; his evidence was a disk at Olympia inscribed with the name of Lycurgus and Iphitus, the founder of the Olympic games. On the other hand, Xenophon[4] dated Lycurgus as contemporary with the Heraclids, by which he presumably meant the conquerors of Laconia. Timaeus, unable to reconcile these contradictions, postulated two men called Lycurgus.[5]

Hellanicus,[6] a historian of the fifth century B.C., ignored him altogether, and attributed the constitution of Sparta to the first two kings after the conquest. It is almost certain that he was not mentioned by Tyrtaeus, for the full text of his poems survived in the classical period and historians cannot have failed to quote any remark of his about so controversial a figure as Lycurgus. As Plutarch,[7] who was a sound scholar, says: 'About Lycurgus the lawgiver it is impossible to make a single statement that is not called in question. His genealogy, his travels, his death, above all his legislation and constitutional activity have been variously recorded and there is a great difference of opinion about his date'.

Some think he was a god. This is supported by the fact that he was later worshipped as such at Sparta[8] and by an ancient Delphic oracle:[9] 'You have come, Lycurgus, to my rich temple,

[1] Plut. *Lyc*. 2.   [2] Plut. *Lyc*. 1.   [3] *Pol*. II. x. 2, 1271b, Plut. *Lyc*. I.
[4] *Resp. Lac*. x. 8.   [5] Plut. *Lyc*. 1.   [6] Strabo, VIII. 366.   [7] *Lyc*. I.
[8] Herod. I. 66, Paus. III. xvi. 5.   [9] Herod. I. 65.

6

dear to Zeus and all who dwell in Olympus. You ask whether I shall divine that you are a god or a man. But I think rather a god, Lycurgus.'

Whether he was a god or a man Lycurgus was a mythical figure. There are, however, two documents commonly associated with his name which are ancient and authentic. One is six (or perhaps ten) lines of Tyrtaeus describing the Spartan constitution. The other is the *rhetra*, an archaic document in prose preserved by Plutarch (via Aristotle).

The Spartans claimed to be and were reputed a very conservative people, and in fact they seem to have preserved their institutions formally intact for centuries, though naturally economic and social changes altered their working, and there were many reforms of the army. In these circumstances the soundest method is to analyse the Spartan constitution of the fifth and fourth centuries B.C.; political events even of the third century are illuminating. Here our evidence is abundant and good. Herodotus gives an elaborate description of the powers of the kings and much incidental material. Thucydides describes the debate in the Spartan assembly which decided for war on Athens in 432, and his narrative illustrates the powers of the kings and ephors. Xenophon, who stayed at Sparta as a young man, wrote a highly uncritical but first-hand account of the Institutions of Sparta in the early fourth century, and also gives much incidental information in his Hellenica. There is an interesting account of a great debate at Sparta shortly after the Persian war in Diodorus,[1] copying Ephorus, who wrote in the middle of the fourth century. Aristotle in the Politics gives a brief but very acute critique of Sparta in the later fourth century; unfortunately his Constitution of the Lacedaemonians has perished. Finally Plutarch has preserved in his Life of Lycurgus much detailed information of very various quality, and in his lives of Agis and Cleomenes a vivid and detailed narrative of the two last constitutional crises in Spartan history.

[1] XI. 50.

III

HELOTS AND PERIOECI: TARAS

THE Lacedaemonian state in historical times consisted of
Laconia and Messenia. It was governed by the citizens of
Sparta, and the remaining population fell into two main classes.
One of these was the Perioeci, who inhabited a number of autonomous cities. They paid rent for certain lands belonging to the
Spartan kings in their territories[1] and their citizens had to serve
in the Spartan army. They had in fact no foreign policy of their
own, but managed their internal affairs. There is little reliable
evidence that in this field they were subject to any control,
except that the Spartans sent an annual resident or judge to the
island city of Cythera,[2] which was obviously of high strategic
importance. Isocrates[3] seems to be wrong in saying that the
ephors could summarily execute a Perioecic citizen; he is mixing
up the Perioeci with the Helots. One Perioecic community, the
Sciritae, who were a rural canton, had the privilege of serving on
the left wing of the Spartan army.[4] The cities were almost consistently loyal to Sparta.

In Roman times there were 24 Perioecic cities,[5] mostly in
the mountains which flank the valley of the Eurotas, Parnon on
the east and Taygetus on the west, but they included Gytheum, the
port of Sparta, and some cities in Messenia. Two cities in this
area, Thuria and Aethaea,[6] were destroyed in the middle of the
fifth century. Another, Asine, had been repeopled with the
inhabitants of Argolic Asine.[7] A fourth, Methone, had been
repeopled by the exiled inhabitants of Nauplia, also in the Argolid.[8]

[1] Xen. Resp. Lac. xv. 3.   [2] Thuc. IV. 53.   [3] XII. 181.   [4] Thuc. V. 67.
[5] Paus. III. xxi. 6–7.   [6] Thuc. I. 101.   [7] Paus. IV. xiv. 3, xxxiv. 9.
[8] Paus. IV. xxxv. 2.

8

The other class was the Helots. The word was derived either from Helos, a destroyed city near the mouth of the Eurotas,[1] or from the word to capture—captives. They are often described as slaves, but their Spartiate masters could not manumit them or sell them overseas. They were in a manner state slaves.[2] They were tied to the soil[3] and cultivated the lands of the Spartiates, probably on a métayage basis, paying half the crop as rent: this is what Tyrtaeus[4] says of the Messenian helots. Plutarch[5] says that 'each man's lot was of such a size that it yielded a rent to the husband of 70 *medimni* of barley, and to his wife 12, and a proportionate quantity of liquids'. The first figure is absurd, and the whole story is tied to the mythical Lycurgan lot, and probably a fiction. They also acted as personal servants to their masters and as their batmen in war.[6] The Spartan government in the fifth and fourth centuries frequently enrolled them as volunteers in the army, giving them freedom; such freed Helots were called New Citizens, Neodamodeis, and had apparently no political rights. They were usually employed overseas or on distant expeditions and were consistently loyal.[7]

Nevertheless the Spartan government was profoundly distrustful of the Helots. Whenever a *levée en masse* of the Spartiates and Perioeci left the country, all adult Helots were also called up for transport services and the like.[8] In her earliest treaty with Tegea Sparta stipulated that Tegea must expel the Messenians[9] and she inserted in the treaty[10] which she made with Athens in 421 a clause that the Athenians would assist her if the slaves revolted, and this was apparently a standard clause in her alliances.[11] Every year the ephors formally declared war on the Helots[12] so that a Spartiate should not be guilty of religious impurity if he killed a Helot out of hand. There was also the institution of the Krypteia,[13]

---

[1] *FGH* 115, F13, Strabo, VIII. 365.   [2] Strabo, 1.c.   [3] Thuc. V. 34.
[4] *Anth. Lyr. Gr.*[3] fr. 5   [5] *Lyc.* 8.   [6] Plut. *Pyrrhus*, 27, *Comp. Lyc. et Num.* 2.
[7] Thuc. V. 34, 67; VII. 19, 58; VIII. 5, Xen. *Hell.* I. iii. 15; III. i. 4, iv. 2, 20; V. ii. 24, Pollux, III. 83.
[8] Herod. IX. 28, Thuc. V. 57, 64.   [9] *Graec. Quaest.* 5.   [10] Thuc. V. 23.
[11] See p. 52.   [12] Plut. *Lyc.* 28.   [13] Plut. *Lyc.* 28.

9

whereby young Spartan warriors were sent out into the country with an iron ration and a dagger, and hid by day and killed the most active Helots by night.[c] Plutarch had to admit that this unpleasant institution was attributed to Lycurgus on the evidence of Aristotle. At times of crisis the Spartan government was utterly ruthless. I quote Thucydides.[1] 'They proclaimed that those of them who claimed to be the best in military affairs should be picked, so that they could be freed, making a test and thinking that those who first claimed to be freed would be the most likely to attack them from pride. So they picked about 2,000 and crowned them and they went round the temples as being freed, and not long afterwards they made them disappear and no-one knew how each had died.'

The ambivalent attitude of the Spartans towards the Helots is no doubt mainly to be explained by their position as a tiny minority ruling a vastly greater number of serfs. We have only one figure; at Plataea (479) there were 5,000 Spartiates of military age, 5,000 Perioeci (no doubt those qualified by their property to serve as hoplites) and 35,000 Helots.[2] The number of Spartiates thereafter dwindled, but the Helots may well have increased.

There is, however, a second explanation which partially accounts for the apparent contradiction. The Messenian Helots rose in rebellion after the great earthquake of 465, and gave substantial assistance to the Athenian landing party which seized Sphacteria in 425 and garrisoned the post for Athens. They achieved their freedom with the aid of Thebes in 370–369. Here some national sentiment evidently survived. But we never hear of any unrest among the Laconian Helots; very few deserted even when the Thebans invaded Laconia in 370. They were no doubt under more regular control than the Messenians, but they must also have had more personal contact with their Spartan landlords. And they probably preserved no memories of their past, when their ancestors had been free men.

[1] IV. 80.   [2] Herod. IX. 28.

10

This picture accords well enough with the various traditional stories of the origins of the Laconian state. According to Ephorus[1] Agis, the second king of Sparta, reduced the other Laconian communities to subjection, and enslaved the people of Helos who alone resisted. According to Plutarch[2] it was Sous, the second king in the other line, who created the Helot system. Pausanias[3] less plausibly puts the enslavement of towns quite near to Sparta much later, Aegys under Archilaus, the eighth king, and Amyclae, Pharis and Geronthrae under his successor Teleclus just before the first Messenian war. It is much more likely that the Spartans first reduced their immediate neighbours in the valley of the Eurotas to serfdom, and then extended their political sway over the mountains to the East and West. The conquest of Messenia by general consent came much later.

Theopompus[4] distinguishes the Messenian helots from those of Laconia, who, he says, were 'the Hellenes who formerly inhabited the country which they now hold', that is 'Achaeans'. It seems unlikely that the Dorian invaders were all concentrated in Sparta, and that the other towns were Achaean. By the fifth century all the inhabitants of Laconia, including the relatively recent conquest of Cynuria, had been Dorianized.[5] Isocrates'[6] version of early Spartan history, that there was a class war among the Dorian conquerors, and that the victorious oligarchs established themselves at Sparta and occupied all the best land, and banished the defeated commons to inferior land in the outlying country, allowing them a very limited degree of self-government, is clearly based on political conditions in fourth century Greece.

It was after the first Messenian war that Sparta founded its first and only successful colony, Taras in Italy. There are stories of earlier colonies in the mythical period, Thera,[7] Lyttos in Crete,[8] Alabanda in Caria,[9] Cibyra,[10] Synnada in Phrygia,[11] and a group of Pisidian cities, Sagalassus,[12] Selge,[13] Amblada,[14] Croton and

---

[1] Strabo, VIII. 365.   [2] *Lyc.* 2.   [3] III. ii. 5–6.   [4] *FGH* 115, F13, 122.
[5] Herod. VIII. 73.   [6] XII. 177–81.   [7] Herod. IV. 147.   [8] Strabo, X. 481.
[9] *B.M.C., Coins of Caria*, p. xxx.   [10] *IGR* III. 500.   [11] *IG* V. i. 452.
[12] Head, *Hist. Num.*[2] 710.   [13] Polyb. V. 76, Strabo, XII. 570.   [14] Head, *Hist. Num.*[2] 705.

Locri in Italy,[1] and the Jews.[2] The story of Taras is given in Strabo,[3] quoting the fifth century Sicilian historian Antiochus and Ephorus, Diodorus,[4] the pseudo-Scymnus,[5] Aristotle[6] and sundry later authors.[7] The colony was said to be the result of a threatened revolution at Sparta. According to Ephorus the Spartans had sworn not to leave the front as long as the Messenian war lasted, but their wives protested. The Spartans sent back the young men, who had not taken the oath (this was in the tenth year of the war), to cohabit with the virgins of Sparta, but their offspring was deemed illegitimate and so was called Partheniae; they plotted with the Helots. In Antiochus' version the Partheniae were children born to Spartan women during the war by Spartiates who stayed at home (and were called Helots). The version of Diodorus calls the bastard class Epeunactoi.

It is difficult to make much of this legendary material, but it seems likely that the colonization of Taras was due to social and economic unrest at the end of the First Messenian War. There was at this time, as we know from Tyrtaeus,[8] economic distress and a demand for redistribution of land, and the colonists of Taras may have been Spartans who were on some ground denied allotments in the newly conquered Messenian land. The date of the colony is given as 706 in Eusebius' chronicle, but this date seems to have no independent validity, but to have been calculated from the Sosibian dates of the Messenian War, given in Eusebius as 746–716.[9] The Partheniae were born in the tenth year of the war, 736, and raised trouble when they were grown up thirty years later.

[1] Paus. III. iii. 1.   [2] I Macc. xii. 5–23. Jos. *Ant. Jud.* XII. 225–27, XIII. 166–70.
[3] VI. 278–280.   [4] VIII. 21.   [5] 330 ff.   [6] *Pol.* V. vii. 2, 1306b.
[7] Dion. Hal. XIX. 1, Paus. X. x. 6–8, III. xii. 5, and Justin, III. iv. 3–11.
[8] Arist. *Pol.* V. vii. 3–4, 1306b–7a.   [9] Eus. *Chron.* II. 81–3, 85, ed. Schoene.

THE KINGS

A T Sparta itself the main elements of the constitution were the
two kings, the *gerusia* or council of elders, the popular
assembly, and the five ephors. Why there were two dynasties
no one knows; the story told to Herodotus[1] was that Argeia, the
wife of Aristodemus, the conqueror of Laconia, had twins and
deliberately mixed them up. The two kings were constitutionally
equal. Descent was by strict primogeniture, except that according
to Herodotus[2] a son born to a king after his accession ranked above
previous sons. No instance is known where this happened.
During a minority the eldest male agnate acted as regent.

Herodotus[3] gives us an interesting description of the constitutional powers of the kings. 'The Spartiates have given the kings
the following privileges, two priesthoods, of Zeus Lacedaemon
and Heavenly Zeus, and to wage war against any country that
they wish, and no Spartiate is to prevent this, otherwise he is
accursed. And when they go to war the kings go first and return
last; and a hundred picked men guard them on campaign. And
they use as many sheep as they wish on expedition. And they
receive the skins and backs of all animals sacrificed. This in war,
and in peace the following privileges are given to them. If there
is any public sacrifice the kings take the first seats at the dinner,
and the serving begins with them, and they receive each a portion
double that of the other guests in everything, and they lead the
libation and they have the skins of the animals sacrificed. And at
every new moon and seventh day of the month each is given a
perfect offering from the treasury of Apollo and a measure of
barley, and a Laconian quart of wine; and they have special front

---

[1] VI. 52.   [2] VII. 3.   [3] VI. 56–60.

seats at all the games. And it is their duty to appoint whomsoever they wish of the citizens as *proxeni* (representatives of foreign states), and each to choose two Pythii: and the Pythii are the envoys to Delphi who are fed by the treasury with the kings. If the kings do not come to dinner two *choinikes* of barley and a *cotyle* of wine are sent to each at his house, and when they are present they are given double of everything, and they receive the same honour when invited to dinner by private persons. They conserve all the oracles that are given, but the Pythii also have knowledge of them. The kings alone judge on the following issues; about a virgin heiress, to whom she should pass, unless her father has betrothed her; about the public roads; and if anyone wishes to adopt a son, he does so before the kings. They sit with the elders, who are 28 in number, in council; and if they do not attend their nearest relatives among the elders have the rights of the kings; the representatives cast two votes and one for themselves.' Thucydides[1] acidly remarks: 'Other Greeks are wrong in saying that the kings of the Lacedaemonians do not each have one vote in addition but two'.

'These are the honours given to the kings by the commonwealth of the Spartiates in their lifetime. When they die horsemen ride all around Laconia announcing the event, and in the city women go around beating cooking pots. So when this occurs, two free persons from each house, a man and a woman, are obliged to go into mourning (literally mutilate themselves) and heavy penalties are imposed on those who do not. . . . When a king of the Lacedaemonians dies, apart from the Spartiates a number of the Perioeci are obliged to go to the funeral. So when they and the Helots and the Spartiates themselves are gathered, there are many thousands, and with the women they beat their brows vigorously and indulge in interminable wailing, and say that the last king who had died was the best; and if one of the kings dies at war, they make an image of him and carry it out on a richly-hung bier.

[1] I. 20.

14

And when they are buried there is no assembly or election for ten days, but they mourn for these days.'

As Herodotus remarks, this is anthropologically interesting, and he points out analogies from barbarian peoples. It will be noted that the civil, judicial and sacred functions of the kings were very limited; jurisdiction in family law in so far as it affected inheritance and managing relations with Delphi. In military affairs the sentence 'they may wage war against any country they wish' was obsolete in Herodotus' day. It seems probable that the change took place in 506, though from the anecdotal character of the evidence it is difficult to be certain.

In that year King Cleomenes 'levied an army from all the Peloponnese (that is from Sparta and her allies), not saying for what purpose he was levying it'. This action he took jointly with his fellow king Demaratus, 'who had not hitherto disagreed with Cleomenes'. When the army arrived at Eleusis and was about to join battle with the Athenians, the Corinthian contingent refused to fight and marched off, and were followed by Demaratus. 'As a result of this dispute a law was passed in Sparta that it should not be lawful for both kings to be present when an army marched out; for hitherto both had been present.'[1] Since the royal prerogative belonged to the kings jointly, the Spartans, by forbidding the kings to march together, effectively if not formally abolished the old royal prerogative.

The resultant situation is correctly stated by Xenophon,[2] when he says that it was the king's right 'to command the army wherever the city sends him'. Henceforth the procedure was that the assembly declared war[3] and the ephors proclaimed the levy.[4] One king was chosen by the assembly[5] and he then exercised absolute strategical authority for the duration of the war. Even in the fifth century the king had authority, during a state of war, to lead out an army against any objective he might choose. In 419

[1] Herod. V. 74–5. [2] *Resp. Lac.* xv. 2.
[3] Thuc. I. 87, Xen. *Hell.* III. ii. 23, IV. vi. 3, VI. iv. 2–3.
[4] Xen. *Hell.* III. ii. 23, 25, v. 6, IV. ii. 9, V. iii. 13, iv. 47, VI. iv. 17, v. 10.
[5] Xen. *Hell.* IV. ii. 9, VI. iv. 18, v. 10.

the Spartans with their allies marched to Leuctra in their own territory under the command of King Agis, 'and no one knew what their objective was, not even the cities from which contingents had been sent'.[1] In the following year, when Agis had in their opinion shown great incompetence at Argos, the Spartans 'laid down a temporary rule which was unprecedented; they chose ten Spartiates as his advisers, without whose consent he should have no authority to lead an army from the city'.[2] From the end of the fifth century he was accompanied by two ephors,[3] but they could only report back and arraign him if they thought fit on his return to the city. The king could not make a final treaty of peace, but could arrange terms and make preliminary settlements.

Aristotle[4] calls the Spartan kingship a perpetual hereditary generalship, but in the hands of an able king it could be and normally was far more than that. The king, it is true, was at home merely one of the elders, and the political leadership of the assembly was in the hands of the ephors. But the advice of a successful general had immense weight with the assembly, and the kings had the advantage of permanency over their potential rivals. A king might, it is true, be baulked by his colleague, but this in fact very rarely happened, since the colleague of an influential king was very often a minor or an ineffective character. In fact, the number of Spartan commoners who swayed Spartan policy can be numbered on the fingers of one hand—the legendary Chilon, Hetoemaridas, Brasidas, Lysander, Antalcidas. The history of Sparta falls naturally into reigns of a series of great kings—Cleomenes I, Archidamus, Agesilaus, Areus, Agis III, Cleomenes IV, Nabis—who left their imprint, for good or ill, on the fortunes of their country.

[1] Thuc. V. 54.
[2] Thuc. V. 63.
[3] Xen. *Resp. Lac.* xiii. 5, *Hell.* II. iv. 36.
[4] *Pol.* III. xiv. 4, 1285b.

V

THE GERUSIA

THE *gerusia* consisted, as we have seen, of 28 members and the two kings. Plutarch[1] gives what are undoubtedly the ancient rules. Members sat for life and candidates had to be sixty years of age or over. The procedure of election was, as Aristotle[2] says, 'childish'. An assembly was called and judges were locked up in a windowless room nearby. The candidates came forward in turn and the people shouted, and the man who got the loudest cheer was elected.[3] There was so far as we know no qualification of property or birth; some phrases of Aristotle might seem to imply the latter, but 'aristocracy' in Greek either means 'the rule of the best' or 'the rule of the nobles', and he probably refers to the former.[d]

The council was the criminal court, judging all capital cases, i.e. those involving death or exile,[4] including impeachment of the kings.[5] They were also the guiding committee of the assembly, and (in early theory at any rate) no motion might be put to the assembly except on their initiative.

Here it is appropriate to quote Tyrtaeus and the *rhetra*. Tyrtaeus[6] wrote: 'Having heard the word of Phoebus they brought home from Pytho the oracles of the god and his sure sayings; that the god-honoured kings who care for the lovely city of Sparta shall initiate council, and the old men, the elders, and then the men of the people, answering with straight sayings' (*rhetrai*). Plutarch stops here but Diodorus goes on: 'shall speak good things and do all things just nor make any (crooked) counsel for this

---

[1] *Lyc.* 26.   [2] *Pol.* II. ix. 25, 1270b.   [3] Plut. *Lyc.* 26.
[4] Xen. *Resp. Lac.* x. 2; Arist. *Pol.* II. ix. 25, 1271a; Plut. *Lyc.* 26.
[5] Paus. III. v. 2.   [6] Plut. *Lyc.* 6.

city, but victory and might shall follow the multitude or the people. For Phoebus spake this to the city about these things.' The Diodorus fragment[1] has the heading: 'The Pythia gave an oracle to Lycurgus on the constitution as follows', and substitutes for Tyrtaeus' opening two lines: 'For the lord Apollo of the silver bow, the far shooter of the golden hair, gave an oracle from his rich shrine'.[c]

The *rhetra* runs something like this;[2] 'To found a temple of Zeus Syllanius and Athene Syllania; to tribe the tribes and obe the obes; to set up a council of elders, thirty with the leaders; to hold assembly from season to season between Babyke and Knakion; so (or they) to introduce and to stand aside (or dismiss); but the denial (or the decision) and the might to be of the people'. It went on (Plutarch says this was a later but very early addition): 'But if the people say a crooked thing, the elders and the leaders to be standers aside (or dismissers)'.[f]

It will be seen that this corresponds very closely with Tyrtaeus, except that he is a royalist, and emphasizes the role of the 'leaders' (the kings). The constitutional part seems to mean that the council called the assembly at fixed periods and put motions (sayings, *rhetrai*) before it, which it could reject or confirm. The council could also, it would seem, veto decisions of the assembly of which it disapproved; it is not explained how the people could make such decisions, seeing that it could only reject or confirm proposals made by the *gerusia*.

The *gerusia* is represented by Isocrates,[3] Demosthenes,[4] Polybius,[5] Dionysius of Halicarnassus[6] and Plutarch,[7] as virtually the governing body of Sparta. In the historical record it is conspicuous by its absence. It supported the ephors against King Anaxandridas,[8] it inconclusively debated the issue of war with Athens in 477,[9] and its members were consulted about the conspiracy of Cinadon.[10] Under Agis IV it exercised

---

[1] VII. 12. 6. [2] Plut. *Lyc.* 6. [3] XII. 154, [4] XX. 107.
[5] VI. 45. [6] II. 14. [7] *Lyc.* 26. [8] Herod. V. 40.
[9] Diod. XI. 50. [10] Xen. *Hell.* III. iii. 8.

its veto and overcame the assembly.[1] It must be remembered, however, that as the criminal court it exercised great political power in the trial of kings and of other military commanders like Sphodrias.

[1] Plut. *Agis*, 11.

VI

THE ASSEMBLY

THE assembly included all adult Spartiates from the age of 20; in the great days of Sparta it could have numbered over 5,000. How far it enjoyed free right of debate is rather doubtful.

Speaking of the Carthaginian constitution Aristotle[1] says: 'Whatever they (the kings and the elders) propose they do not only allow the people to listen to the decision of the rulers, but they are entitled to judge and anyone who likes is allowed to speak against the proposals; which is not the case in the other constitutions' (those of Sparta and Crete). Speaking of Crete he furthermore says: 'They all share in the assembly, but it has no power except to ratify the decisions of the elders and *cosmi*'.[2] In this chapter he generally notes divergencies between Spartan and Cretan institutions, if they existed, and it may be inferred that on this point Cretan and Spartan practice agreed. Taken quite literally Aristotle would seem to be saying that the assembly merely listened to and formally confirmed motions of the kings and elders. This is so clearly untrue that Aristotle cannot have meant it. When he says that the Cretan assembly could only ratify motions, he must mean ratify or reject. Similarly when he implies that Spartan and Cretan people could only listen to the proposals of the magistrates, but they (the members of the assembly) might not judge and that ordinary members were not allowed to speak against the proposals, he cannot be excluding a vote of the assembly, but is stating that ordinary members could not make speeches and criticize—much less propose amendments.

The reports on popular assemblies at Sparta show that there was debate. In 475 (according to Diodorus;[3] a more probable

---

[1] *Pol.* II. xi. 6, 1273a.   [2] *Pol.* II. x. 7, 1272a.   [3] XI. 50.

date is two years earlier) a distinguished elder, Hetoemaridas, persuaded the *gerusia* and the people to reject a proposal for war against Athens. In the assembly which decided for war in 432 'the opinions of the majority were in the same sense, that the Athenians were doing wrong and that war must be made forthwith', but King Archidamus then made a speech advocating delay, and finally an ephor, Sthenelaidas, spoke strongly for war.[1] Different opinions were clearly expressed but we unfortunately do not know whether the earlier speakers were ordinary members of the assembly or elders or ephors. In the debate in 371 whether to attack Thebes forthwith a certain Prothous urged a more deliberate procedure, but the assembly neglected his advice and voted for war at once.[2] Once again we do not know what position, if any, Prothous held. In 242 when the ephor Lysander proposed the abolition of debts and the redistribution of the land, he himself spoke to the measure, and so did the two kings, Agis in favour and Leonidas against, and also Mandrocleidas and Agesilaus.[3] Agesilaus was certainly not ephor, since he held the office next year,[4] and Mandrocleidas is not stated to have been ephor, but was prosecuted with Lysander by the next board of ephors for having 'voted' the bill, and was presumably its joint promoter.[5] Both were elderly men and may have been members of the *gerusia*.

Finally, there is an anecdote recorded by Aeschines.[6] A clever orator of dissolute life was speaking in the Spartan assembly, and the Spartans seemed likely to vote according to his advice, when an elder, indignant that they should listen to so bad a character even if he gave good advice, called upon an inarticulate but virtuous citizen to express the same views. Here the virtuous Spartan is clearly not an elder or office-holder nor is apparently the dissolute Spartan. The anecdote is not very trustworthy evidence, and is the more suspect as it appears in Plutarch[7] in a

---

[1] Thuc. I. 79–86.   [2] Xen. *Hell*. VI. iv. 2–3.   [3] Plut. *Agis*, 9–10.
[4] Plut. *Agis*, 12.   [5] Plut. *Agis*, 12.   [6] I. 180–1.
[7] *Mor*. 801bc.

different form in which the bad citizen (called Demosthenes) expresses a sound opinion (or makes a sound proposal) but the assembly rejects it, and the ephors then choose one of the elders by lot to make the same speech.

This evidence proves that kings and elders might speak against the motion—there is no recorded instance of an ephor doing so—and does not exclude the possibility that ordinary citizens might also speak for or against, perhaps at the invitation of the elders or the ephors. Only in Plutarch's version of Aeschines' anecdote is there any suggestion that a private member might propose a motion, and even here the language is ambiguous. Aristotle appears to be right in implying that the assembly could only vote yes or no, and that there was no power of amendment by private citizens.

The most striking feature of the later evidence is, however, that the kings and elders never appear as making a proposal or as summoning or presiding in the assembly. These roles are always taken by the ephors, or an ephor. In 432 it is the ephor Sthenelaidas who, in virtue of his office, puts the question to the vote.[1] On several occasions it is the ephors who convene an assembly to hear foreign envoys.[2] Votes of the assembly are expressed in the form: 'It was resolved by the ephors and the assembly'.[3] Epitadeus moved the *rhetra* known by his name 'having become ephor'.[4] Finally, when King Agis IV wished to abolish debts and redistribute the land, it was Lysander, one of the ephors, who moved the *rhetra* in the *gerusia* and subsequently in the assembly.[5]

There are two incidents on which we have fuller information, those of 477 (?) and of 242. On the former occasion, 'when the *gerusia* had been convened they deliberated about the war against Athens for the leadership at sea. And similarly when the general assembly was convened the younger men and most of the elders were enthusiastic to recover the leadership. . . . And when

[1] Thuc. I. 87.   [2] Xen. *Hell*. II. ii. 19, V. ii. 11.   [3] Ib. III. ii. 23, IV. vi. 3.
[4] Plut. *Agis*, 5.   [5] Plut. *Agis*, 8–9.

practically all the citizens were set on this course, and the *gerusia* was in session on the question, no one hoped that anyone would dare to advocate any other course. But a member of the *gerusia*, Hetoemaridas by name, a Heraclid by descent and esteemed among the citizens for his high character, tried to advocate leaving the Athenians in the leadership . . . and contrary to expectation he persuaded the *gerusia* and the people.'[1]

The interesting point about this story is that before the *gerusia* had come to any decision the assembly was convened and debated the question. Who convened the assembly? From the evidence already cited and from the next case to be discussed there can be little doubt that it was the ephors.

'Agis, having arranged that Lysander should be made ephor, forthwith introduced a *rhetra* through him into the *gerusia* . . . and when the *rhetra* had been proposed and the elders did not agree in their opinions Lysander convened an assembly and himself spoke to the citizens.'[2] There follows an account of the debate in which Mandrocleidas and Agesilaus and finally Agis himself spoke for the motion, and the other king, Leonidas, raised objections. 'As a result the majority followed Agis, and the rest urged Leonidas not to desert them, and by their pleas and persuasion they prevailed upon the elders, with whom lay the power in making the preliminary resolution, to such effect that those who voted against the *rhetra* were in a majority of one.' This meant that the *rhetra* was lost.[3]

Once again we may observe that a bill was put to the assembly before the *gerusia* had approved it, and in this case it is stated to have been an ephor who both proposed the bill in the *gerusia* and convened the assembly and introduced the bill there.

Does Agis' manœuvre of getting Lysander as ephor to introduce the *rhetra* imply that only an ephor was constitutionally entitled to propose a bill? Not necessarily, I would suggest. It was, it would appear from the evidence cited above, customary

---

[1] Diod. XI. 50. [2] Plut. *Agis*, 8–9. [3] Plut. *Agis.* 11.

for the ephors to convene the assembly and put motions to it, and Agis may have preferred to conform to constitutional convention. In the second place, the kings, according to the *rhetra*, were merely members of the *gerusia*, and it was the *gerusia* as a whole that decided what proposals to put to the assembly. If then Agis had proposed his *rhetra* in the *gerusia* himself he would have had to win a majority in that conservative body before the question could be put to the people. It was very unlikely that he would be successful in achieving this. His best policy was to get the *rhetra* before the people and hope that the pressure of popular opinion would intimidate the *gerusia*—and this only an ephor could do.

In neither case is it clear whether the assembly took a formal vote before the *gerusia* had made its decision, but there is a curious difference in the conclusions of the two stories, which suggests that in the one case the assembly did vote and in the other did not. Under Agis IV the negative vote of the *gerusia* was decisive; the *rhetra* was killed. In 477 B.C. Hetoemaridas had to persuade both the *gerusia* and the assembly to reject the motion. This suggests that in the former case the people had made a crooked decision, and the *gerusia* was therefore in a position to exercise its right of veto under the rider. In the latter case the assembly had not voted, and the only action which the *gerusia* could take was to refuse to sponsor the motion. This left the ephors free to put their motion to the people, which they apparently did, but Hetoemaridas persuaded the assembly to reject it.

It would be possible to argue that the ephors, though they could introduce a motion into the assembly for discussion, could not put it to the vote without a formal resolution by the *gerusia*. Under this hypothesis Lysander's *rhetra* had to be dropped because the *gerusia* refused to bring it forward; this is apparently what Plutarch thought when he used the expression 'with whom lay the probouleutic power'. It is more difficult on this hypothesis to explain why Hetoemaridas had to persuade the people as well as the *gerusia*. One can only suggest that he addressed them

24

informally to explain and justify the decision of the *gerusia* not to bring the bill forward.

The important fact remains, however, that the ephors could initiate a debate in the assembly without the consent of the *gerusia*, and in view of the fact that they had, as Thucydides emphasizes, the constitutional right of putting a proposal to the vote, it seems likely that they could not only introduce a proposal on their own initiative, but put it to the vote. This would explain how the people could make a crooked decision.

VII

THE EPHORS

W E now come to the ephors, who are not mentioned in the *rhetra* or in Tyrtaeus, and whose origin was attributed by some[1] to Lycurgus and by others[2] to Theopompus and by Plato[3] either to Lycurgus or to a 'third saviour'. There were five annual ephors, one of whom was eponymous (gave his name to the year). They normally acted together and in cases of difference of policy the dissidents were bound by a majority vote. As Critias said to Theramenes;[4] 'In Lacedaemon if one of the ephors should undertake to find fault with the government and to oppose its measures, instead of yielding to the majority, do you not think that he would be regarded not only by the ephors themselves but by the rest of the city as deserving the severest punishment?' They were elected by the assembly 'in a very childish way'[5] and any Spartan citizen (probably over 30) was eligible. Aristotle[6] assures us that quite poor and undistinguished men were often elected; no one could hold office twice.

Their powers in Laconia were very extensive and varied. They annually declared war on the Helots[7] and could execute them without trial.[8] They could discipline and fine all other magistrates.[9] They had disciplinary powers over all citizens, issuing a proclamation when they entered upon office that they should 'shave their upper lips and obey the laws';[10] they judged

---

[1] Herod. I. 65, Xen. *Resp. Lac.* viii. 1–3.   [2] Arist. *Pol.* V. xi. 2, 1313a, Plut. *Lyc.* 7.
[3] *Laws*, 692a, *Ep.* VIII. 354b.
[4] Xen. *Hell.* II. iii. 34; cf. II. iv. 29, where it was enough for Pausanias to persuade three of the ephors.
[5] Arist. *Pol.* II. ix. 23, 1270b.   [6] *Pol.* II. ix. 19, 23, 1270b.   [7] Plut. *Lyc.* 28.
[8] Isocrates, XII. 181; see above, p. 8.
[9] Xen. *Resp. Lac.* viii. 4; Arist. *Pol.* II. ix. 26, 1271a.   [10] Plut. *Cleom.* 9.

(sitting separately) all civil causes.[1] They virtually conducted foreign policy, receiving envoys (actual treaties had to go to the assembly). They presided normally in the assembly.[2] They seem also to have presided in the council. After approaching the king by themselves the ephors then consulted the *gerusia* and enlisted its support in persuading King Anaxandridas to take a second wife.[3] They were present and voted when King Pausanias was tried.[4] When the conspiracy of Cinadon was revealed they did not dare to call a meeting of the 'little assembly' (probably a popular term for the *gerusia*), but consulted individual elders.[5] Under Agis IV Lysander the ephor introduced a *rhetra* into the *gerusia*.[6]

It is their relations with the kings which are most interesting. By an ancient custom the ephors on a certain night each ninth year watched the skies, and if they saw a shooting star announced that there was something wrong about the kings.[7] In the presence of the kings all others rose but ephors remained seated.[8] If the ephors summoned a king he refused twice and then he had to go.[9] They could fine the king. Archidamus was fined by the ephors for marrying a short wife; 'for she will bear us not kings but kinglets'.[10] Agesilaus was fined because 'he was acquiring the commons citizens as his own' by his ingratiating ways.[11] The ephors could even arrest a king—'it is lawful for the ephors to do this to the king'.[12] If the king was impeached before the council, the ephors sat and voted.[13] Finally, they exchanged a monthly oath with the kings, 'for the king that he would rule according to the established laws of the city, and for the city that if he was true to his oath they would maintain his kingdom unshaken'.[14]

It is evident that the political development of Sparta was abnormal. In most Greek cities the first stage was that the nobles

[1] Arist. *Pol.* III. i. 10, 1275b.   [2] See pp. 22 ff.   [3] Herod. V. 40.
[4] Paus. III. v. 2.   [5] Xen. *Hell.* III. iii. 8.   [6] Plut. *Agis*, 8.
[7] Plut. *Agis*, 11.   [8] Xen. *Resp. Lac.* xv. 6.   [9] Plut. *Cleom.* 10.
[10] Plut. *Ages.* 2.   [11] Plut. *Ages.* 5.
[12] Thuc. I. 131. Cf. Plut. *Agis*, 18–19.
[13] Paus. III. v. 2. Cf. Plut. *Agis*, 19.   [14] Xen. *Resp. Lac.* xv. 7.

abolished the kingship or, as at Athens, converted it into a magistracy of minor importance, and the council of nobles became the governing body. Later there often followed a struggle between the commons and the nobles. At Sparta the kings and the nobles seem to have compromised. There hereditary kingship survived and the kings retained the military command undiminished; but at home they kept only their landed wealth, their honours, their sacred functions and a vestigial jurisdiction. Otherwise they became ordinary members of the council of elders; it would seem likely, however, that in view of their prestige they remained the leaders of the aristocracy, and were regarded as such by the people.

When the people became restive they also proceeded in an unusual way. They did not attempt to overthrow the kingship. Instead they elected annually a board of five ephors to champion their rights. These ephors claimed powers to control and discipline the kings, and they also held meetings of the people and enacted resolutions for which they claimed the force of law.

They seem also to have reformed the *gerusia*, which had presumably hitherto been a council of nobles. The *rhetra* specified that the number of elders was to be fixed at 28, and it was probably at this date that popular election was introduced and commoners made admissible.

The *rhetra* with its rider seems to represent a settlement or settlements of the struggle. The sole initiative of the council is affirmed —which implies that it had been challenged—but the right of the people to accept or reject its proposals is solemnly admitted. In the rider the possibility of legislation initiated by some other authority than the council is tacitly admitted, but the council is given a power of veto. The ephors, being at this time a revolutionary body, are ignored in a document evidently drafted by the nobility.

If this development is unique among Greek cities it bears a certain resemblance to the struggle of the orders at Rome. The

28

kingship had, it is true, been abolished at Rome, but the two consuls possessed virtually regal powers, in particular, like the Spartan kings, untrammelled authority *militiae*, while at home they were the leaders of the senate, the aristocratic council of elders. The tribunes of the plebs are compared by Cicero[1] to the ephors, and were like them commoners elected annually by the people to champion their rights. They claimed the right of resisting and even of arresting and executing the consuls, and they also called assemblies of the people and proposed measures to them, for which they claimed the force of law. The nobility resisted this claim and, it would appear, asserted in the *patrum auctoritas* the right of the senate to approve or disallow measures voted by the people.

There is no need to believe Cleomenes III's account of the origin of the ephorate,[2] which is highly tendentious. 'When the Messenian war proved to be long, the kings, since their campaigns abroad left them no time to give justice themselves, chose some of their friends and left them behind to serve in their stead for the citizens, calling them ephors, and they continued at first to be servants of the kings, but gradually drew power into their own hands. . . . The one who first strengthened the office and extended it was Asteropus, who became ephor many generations later.' Asteropus is otherwise unknown and his name, the 'star gazer', suggests that he was the mythical founder of the stargazing rite.

There is no need either to believe that ephors were a primitive Dorian institution. Ephors, it is true, are found in later times in the cities of the Perioeci,[3] in Messene,[4] in Thera,[5] in Cyrene,[6] in Euhesperides,[7] and in the Italian Heraclea,[8] but these may all be later imitations of the Spartan office.

It has been claimed that a list of eponymous ephors from 754 was preserved. In fact, Plutarch[9] states that the first board of

---

[1] *de Rep*. III. 58, *de Legibus*, III. 16.   [2] Plut. *Cleom*. 10. See note bb.
[3] *IG* V. i. 931–2, 961–2, 964–6, 976, 1110–11, 1144–6, 1331. 1336.
[4] Polyb. IV. 4.   [5] *IG* XII. iii. 322, 326, 330, 336.
[6] Arist. *fr*. 611. 18, *SEG* IX. 1 § 5.   [7] *SEG* XVIII. 772.   [8] *IG* XIV. 645.   [9] *Lyc*. 7.

ephors, led by Elatus, held office 130 years after Lycurgus, and Eusebius[1] says that the ephorate was established when Sparta had been ruled by kings for 350 years, while Diogenes Laertius[2] puts the first ephors in the sixth Olympiad. These dates all tally with 754 on the Apollodoran system, but there is no evidence for a list. It is worthy of note that the first recorded use of the ephorate for dating is in the fifth century, in a Laconian inscription[3] and in Thucydides,[4] and that events in early Spartan history are always dated by Olympiads and Athenian archons. The date was probably calculated as being in Theopompus' reign, when the Messenian war (Apollodoran dates, 756–737) had been in progress for a few years, on the basis of the fact that the ephors were originally created to represent the kings in their absence during the Messenian war.

Modern historians have sometimes spoken of the policy of the ephors or the tradition of the ephors, as if there were some mystic continuity between successive boards, and have assumed automatic hostility between the ephors and any prominent king.[5] In point of fact there was no continuity of policy between boards. We know of one case where a board which had signed a peace treaty with Athens was succeeded by another which did its best to wreck it,[5] and the occasional violent fluctuations in Spartan policy imply that this happened not infrequently. Roughly speaking the ephors represented the will of the majority. When feeling was strongly in one direction there would be continuity of policy. When opinion was equally divided, or fluctuated, the ephors reflected this instability. When a king like Agesilaus was carrying out a policy which all Spartans approved, the ephors gave him their full support. When a king like Archidamus was fighting the tide of public opinion, he would often be over-ruled or frustrated by the ephors.

[1] Eus. *Chron.* II. 78, 81, ed. Schoene.   [2] I. 68.   [3] *IG Dial. Sel.* 19.
[4] II. 2.   [5] Thuc. V. 36.

30

VIII

THE DATE OF THE *RHETRA*

THE poem of Tyrtaeus begins without a subject, but Plutarch implies that it was Theopompus and Polydorus. This is a slightly unusual pair as genealogically it is a generation out. Plutarch, who had the full text of Tyrtaeus before him (or if not Plutarch, Aristotle), probably found the names in the preceding lines of Tyrtaeus. The *rhetra* was therefore in existence under these two kings. Plutarch, following Aristotle, attributed the last clause of the *rhetra* to these two kings and the main body to Lycurgus. Tyrtaeus regards the whole constitution as their work.

Aristotle could not understand why the last clause of the *rhetra* was needed. He explained that 'later on when the multitude by subtractions and additions twisted the motions and forced them into a worse form, the kings Theopompus and Polydorus added this to the *rhetra*'.[1] But this, as he himself says elsewhere, is what the Spartan assembly could never do.

It may be asked why Aristotle separated the last clause of the *rhetra* from the main body. The reason is plain. Aristotle knew the *rhetra* was the work of Lycurgus, *c.* 776, but Tyrtaeus quoted what seemed to be the *rhetra* as being enacted under Theopompus and Polydorus two generations—actually nearly three long reigns—later. Moreover, the last clause seemed to contradict the rest of the law.

The council was reformed as stated in the *rhetra*, and beside the 'tribes' the 'obes' were recognized. The 'tribes' were the three Dorian clans common to all Doric cities, the Hylleis, Dymanes and Pamphyli. The 'obes' were apparently villages, and were probably five in number. In Herodotus'[2] day it would

[1] The words are Plutarch's, *Lyc.* 6.   [2] III. 55, IX. 53.

seem that each obe manned a regiment; he mentions Pitane, a village of Sparta, and a Pitanate regiment. Thucydides[1] in his nasty way remarks: 'the other Greeks are wrong' in saying 'that they have a Pitanate regiment, which has never existed yet', and verbally he was probably right. Aristotle[2] recorded the five regiments as Edolos, Sinis, Arimas, Ploas and Messoages, whereas the recorded obes are Mesoa, Pitane, Conoura, Limnae and probably Amyclae.[3][h] Their number corresponds with that of the ephors and of the *agathoergoi*[4] and of the five arbitrators who decided the issues over Salamis *c.* 570.[5]

Tyrtaeus mentions the 'tribes' as military formations,[i] and it has been argued that the *rhetra* must therefore be later than the second Messenian war. But he may have been alluding to the first Messenian war, or the military organization may have remained tribal and not 'obal' for awhile; the old cavalry always numbered 300.[6] The importance of this change is not obvious, but on the analogy of other states it may have afforded the opportunity for enrolling in the full citizen body commoners or immigrants who did not belong to the old tribes.

The ephorate was created and became a check on the royal power in the reign of Theopompus.[7] Polydorus, rather than Theopompus, was perhaps the wise king who yielded. 'The Spartans honour King Polydorus so highly that his likeness is engraved on the seal with which the magistrates seal everything that requires it.'[8] For what it is worth, he was reputed to have been assassinated by a Spartan noble, Polemarchus, and was honoured by later generations for his mild judgments.[9]

There is one limiting factor. It is highly improbable that the warriors of Sparta would have imposed their will on the kings before the hoplite, or heavily armed infantryman, superseded the aristocratic cavalryman. Archaeological evidence suggests that

[1] I. 20.   [2] *fr.* 541.
[3] *IG* V. I. 566, 675–6, 682, 684–6, 688, Paus. III. xvi. 9, *IG* V. i. 26.
[4] Herod. I. 67.   [5] Plut. *Solon,* 10.
[6] Herod. VIII. 124, Thuc. V. 72, Xen. *Resp. Lac.* iv. 3.
[7] Arist. *Pol.* V. xi. 2, 1313a.   [8] Paus. III. xi. 10.   [9] Paus. III. iii. 2–3.

throughout Greece this change took place before 700. Hoplite arms and armour are represented on vases as early as the middle of the eighth century, but warriors fighting in close formation do not appear until early in the seventh century. This, however, is probably because the hoplite phalanx is more difficult to portray and less effective artistically than two or four warriors.[1] If Epaminondas was right in dating the end of the second Messenian war *c.* 600, the first Messenian war would have been *c.* 700–680, and might well have been fought by hoplites. The period after the first Messenian war seems to have been one of acute social unrest. According to tradition the foundation of Taras took place at this time and was the result of some violent conflict.[2] Tyrtaeus recorded that there was at this time a demand for redistribution of land.[3] If the Spartan hoplites had recently fought and won a twenty years' war and were suffering from economic distress as a result, it is not unnatural that they should have asserted their rights against the kings and nobles at this time.

It may be that the festival of the Carneia was founded to celebrate the end of civil strife. It was, according to Sosibius, founded in the 26th Olympiad (676–673), and the dates for the foundation of Greek festivals seem generally to have been sound, being based on victor lists; the Carneonicae were collected by Hellanicus in the fifth century.[4] It is of interest to note that in this festival the three Dorian tribes, each divided into nine phratries, played a part; evidently the five new obes were not yet used for sacred purposes at any rate.[5]

---

[1] A. M. Snodgrass, *JHS* LXXXV (1965), 110 ff.; I accept the author's evidence, but draw different conclusions from it.
[2] See page 12, above.   [3] Arist. *Pol.* V. vii. 3-4, 1306 b-7a.
[4] Athenaeus, XIV. 635e.   [5] Athenaeus, IV. 141ef.

IX

THE DISCIPLINE

THE famous discipline of the Spartans was attributed to Lycurgus. It is undoubtedly very ancient fundamentally and has close analogies with the customs of many primitive warrior tribes throughout the world. The discipline is described by Xenophon[1] and Plutarch.[2]

From the close resemblance between the institutions of Sparta and those of the Dorian cities of Crete it was inevitably conjectured that one had borrowed from the other. Herodotus[3] and Ephorus[4] argued for the priority of Crete. Aristotle[5] said: 'It is probable and is stated that in general the constitution of the Lacedaemonians is a copy of that of the Cretans', and cited the story that Lycurgus travelled in Crete before his legislation. Strabo[6] controverted Ephorus, but Plutarch[7] followed Aristotle. In reality the resemblance is clearly due to a common primitive origin.

Each infant was examined shortly after birth by the 'elders of the tribesmen', who either passed it or, if it was weakly or deformed, ordered it to be thrown over a special cliff.[8] At 8 the boy was enrolled in a 'herd' under a senior Spartiate; it is not clear whether he still lived at home at this stage.[9] At 13 he passed into another series of 'herds'; the year groups were called various curious archaic names (mostly known from Roman inscriptions and later *scholia*), *rhobidai, mikichizomenoi, propaides* (or *hatropampaides*), *paides* (or *pratopampaides*), *melleirenes, eirenes.*[10]

---

[1] *Resp. Lac.* ii–iv.   [2] *Inst. Lac.* 4 ff., *Lyc.* 16–7.   [3] I. 65.
[4] Strabo, X. 481ff.   [5] *Pol.* II. x. 1–2, 1271b.   [6] loc. cit.
[7] *Lyc.* 4.   [8] Plut. *Lyc.* 16.   [9] Plut. *Lyc.* 16.
[10] *IG* V. i. 273–334, *AJP* LXII (1941), 499 ff.

During these years they were looked after by prefects, chosen from the senior age group, the *eirenes*, under the general supervision of a magistrate, the *paedonomus*.[1]

The training was mainly athletic and military, but there was singing of traditional songs, and no doubt Homer and the Spartan poets were read. The boys lived very hard—they slept in dormitories on rushes which they had to cut themselves without knives, received one garment a year, and very meagre rations. They were not allowed baths (of course they could bathe in the river, but the Eurotas is very cold in winter).[2] To supplement their meagre diet they were encouraged to steal food and punished if they were caught for being so clumsy.[3] Contemporary Greeks found this funny and quizzed Spartans about it.[4] Girls received a similar athletic and musical training and like the boys held public competitions; other Greeks were shocked at girls appearing naked in public.[5]

Some of the tests to which the boys were put were very brutal. Notorious was the game of stealing cheeses from the altar of Artemis Orthia; the boys had to run a gauntlet of flogging under which not a few died.[6]

According to the romantic later versions, the young men went through a form of raping the girls of their choice; the pair cohabited clandestinely, often until the first child was born, when they set up house.[7] Of course, actually marriages were arranged by the parents in the usual Greek way. The age of marriage was by Greek standards late—about 20 for men and not much lower for women. The rule was monogamy and divorce was rare, but the wife could cohabit temporarily with a Spartiate of her husband's choice.[8] It would appear that the children went to the real father, but no doubt any other arrangements could be made.

[1] Xen. *Resp. Lac.* ii. 2; Plut. *Lyc.* 17.
[2] Xen. *Resp. Lac.* ii. 1–5; Plut. *Inst. Lac.* 5–12.
[3] Xen. *Resp. Lac.* ii. 6–8; Plut. *Lyc.* 17–18.
[4] Xen. *Anab.* IV. vi. 14–5.   [5] Xen. *Resp. Lac.* i. 4; Plut. *Lyc.* 14–5.
[6] Plut. *Lyc.* 18; *Inst. Lac.* 40; Paus. III. xvi. 10, VIII. xxiii. 1.
[7] Plut. *Lyc.* 15.   [8] Xen. *Resp. Lac.* i. 7–9; Plut. *Lyc.* 15.

At the age of 20 the young Spartan became eligible for one of the famous dining clubs (*pheiditia, syssitia*).[1] Membership averaged fifteen, and one blackball barred election.[2] There were no doubt smart and less eligible clubs, but a young Spartiate could certainly get into one or another of them. Here he ate every day a substantial but dreary diet of barley bread, a peculiarly nauseous haggis (the speciality of Sparta, once cooked by an imported cook for Dionysius the tyrant of Syracuse and one of the kings of Pontus —they both thought it awful),[3] wine (a limited ration and no treating) and a very exiguous dessert of figs or cheese. Members could bring game to the mess and other luxuries. There were Helot cooks and waiters.

Each member paid a subscription. It was according to Plutarch[4] one *medimnus* of barley monthly, eight *choes* of wine, five *minae* of cheese, two and a half *minae* of figs, and a little money for dessert. Another authority, Dicaearchus,[5] says it was one and a half Attic *medimni* of barley, 11 or 12 *choes* of wine, a small quantity of figs and cheese, and 10 Aeginetan obols for meat. The kings each belonged to a mess, receiving double rations, and if absent were served their rations at home, but not double.[6] Curiously enough the heir apparent was not put through the discipline; it was considered remarkable that Agesilaus, being a collateral, had done the course.[7]

All Spartiates were in theory 'peers',[8] but in fact there were men of good family who had more political influence than their fellows,[9] and there were considerable inequalities of wealth. Some families were rich,[10] rich enough to breed race-horses. Pausanias[11] declares that 'after the Persian invasion the Lacedaemonians were the most enthusiastic of all the Greeks in horse

[1] Herod. I. 65; Xen. *Resp. Lac.* v. 2–6; Plut. *Lyc.* 10, 12; *Inst. Lac.* 1–3; Arist. *Pol.* II. ix. 31–2, 1271a.
[2] Plut. *Lyc.* 12.　　[3] Plut. *Lyc.* 12; *Inst. Lac.* 2.　　[4] *Lyc.* 12.
[5] Athenaeus, IV. 141c.　　[6] Herod. VI. 57, Xen. *Resp. Lac.* xv. 4, Plut. *Lyc.* 12.
[7] Plut. *Ages.* 1.
[8] ὅμοιοι, Xen. *Resp. Lac.* x. 7, xiii. 1, 7; *Hell.* III. iii. 5; *Anab.* IV. vi. 14.
[9] Thuc. V. 15.　　[10] Herod. VI. 61–2, VII. 134, Xen. *Resp. Lac.* v. 3.
[11] VI. ii. 1–2, cf, i. 7.

breeding' and mentions six Spartans who won the chariot race at the Olympia during the fifth century, and an inscription[1] of the same period records many victories of a Spartan horse breeder in other races. Others could scarcely pay their mess bills. The common education, however, and the common meals produced a genuine equality, and poor and obscure Spartiates could readily rise by merit. Lysander, of noble—indeed Heraclid—descent, but too poor to pay his own school fees, rose to be the leader of the Spartan state.[2] Brasidas by his energy in a very minor command in Laconia[3] caught the attention of the authorities, who appointed him adviser to Cnemus, commander in the north-west, and his successor Alcidas,[4] and later gave him a force of Helots and mercenaries, with which he achieved brilliant successes in Thrace.

It was a condition of Spartiate citizenship that a boy should undergo the training[5] and a man should pay his mess bill,[6] and in course of time many failed and became Inferiors.[7] It is fairly certain that they had no political rights, and as they could hardly afford uniform and armour presumably did not serve in the army.

There was also a mysterious class called the Mothakes or Mothones. They are distinguished in the dictionaries as 'foster brothers of free boys'.[8] According to Phylarchus[9] 'the Mothakes are foster brothers of the Lacedaemonians. For each of the citizen boys . . . choose some one, some two, some several foster brothers for themselves. The Mothakes then are free, but not Lacedaemonians, and they share in all the education. They say that Lysander was one of them, the man who defeated the Athenians at sea; and he was made a citizen for valour.' Aelian[10] states that 'Callicratidas and Gylippus and Lysander were called Mothakes in Lacedaemon. This was the name of the slaves of the rich whom

<hr/>

[1] *IG Dial. Sel.* 19.   [2] See p. 38.   [3] Thuc. II. 25.
[4] Thuc. II. 85–6, 93, III. 69, 76, 79.   [5] Plut. *Inst. Lac.* 2.
[6] Arist. *Pol.* II. ix. 31, 1271a.
[7] ὑπομείονες—the word only occurs in Xen. *Hell.* III. iii. 6. and is not explained.
[8] See *Historia* XI (1962), pp. 427–8; cf. Plut. *Cleom.* 8.   [9] Athenaeus, VI. 271ef.
[10] *Var. Hist.* XII. 43.

their fathers sent out with their sons to compete in the gymnasia. Lycurgus, who allowed this, granted Laconian citizenship to those who persevered in the training of the boys.'

Now Lysander was a Heraclid[1] and Gylippus the son of a very distinguished Spartiate, Cleandridas, who was exiled in 445.[2] Their common fate was to be very poor.[3] Mothakes therefore were not slaves but sons of inferiors.

The whole system of the discipline is obviously very primitive, but whether it was always applied to the nobility and included even the humblest Spartiate is more doubtful. The poems of Alcman (Apollodoran dates 654–611) suggest a gay and cultivated aristocratic society such as certainly did not exist in the fifth century. One may suspect the discipline was tightened and made obligatory on all after the second Messenian war.

The discipline eventually played a part in killing Laconian art which had hitherto been flourishing. Not that the Spartiates had ever been artists, but they had been liberal and tasteful patrons. During the fifth century they ceased to demand beautiful things, just as they ceased to patronize poetry—Alcman is the last foreign poet who lived in Sparta, and Tyrtaeus the last Spartan poet. The fine Laconian painted pottery declined after the middle of the sixth century, but so did the Corinthian; both yielded to the competition of Attic. Fine ivories ceased about the same period, but quite good bronze figurines continued to be produced into the fifth century and so did quite competent sculpture. Public building also went on. The famous throne of Apollo at Amyclae was commissioned in the late sixth century and the Persian Stoa soon after the Persian wars. After this there is nothing.[4]

According to Xenophon[5] and all later authorities,[6] Lycurgus forbade the possession by any Spartiate of gold and silver, and instituted a coinage of iron spits. Such a law cannot of course have been enacted at the time of the constitutional settlement

[1] Plut. *Lys.* 2.   [2] Plut. *Pericles*, 22, *Nicias*, 28.
[3] Plut. *Lys.* 2. Cleandridas' property was no doubt confiscated when he was exiled.
[4] *CQ* XII (1962), 156–8.   [5] *Resp. Lac.* vii.   [6] e.g. Plut. *Lyc.* 9.

early in the seventh century, as coinage had not yet been invented, and no specific law may have been laid down until the beginning of the fourth century. All we can say with certainty is that Sparta never issued silver coins until the reign of Areus I (309–265), and that the primitive iron spits, commonly used in many Greek cities before the introduction of coinage, remained in use at Sparta down into the fourth century.[1] Foreign coins, however, seem to have circulated. King Agis was fined 10,000 drachmae in 421,[2] and Archidamus and Agesilaus were also fined.[3] After Aegospotami there was such an influx of gold and silver that the conservatives tried to revive the Lycurgan ban, and it was decided that the treasury might hold gold and silver but not individuals.[4] Nevertheless, part of the Spartiate's mess contribution was in Aeginetan obols.[5]

[1] Xen. *Resp. Lac.* vii. 5.   [2] Thuc. V. 63.   [3] Plut. *Ages.* 2, 5.
[4] Plut. *Lys.* 17.   [5] Athenaeus, IV. 141c.

X

THE LAND SYSTEM

WE now come to the Spartan system of land tenure. The whole subject is limpid in Plutarch's Life of Lycurgus, but fades away in authors of the fourth century and earlier. Plutarch's story is that Lycurgus redistributed all the land into 30,000 lots for the Perioeci and 9,000 for the Spartiates, all exactly equal. 'Some say Lycurgus distributed 6,000 and Polydorus afterwards added 3,000, others that he did half the 9,000 and Lycurgus the other half.'[1] Every Spartiate infant thereafter received a lot at birth.[2] The figures are suspect because King Agis in 242 projected a distribution of 4,500 lots to Spartiates and 15,000 to Perioeci,[3] half the original total because of the loss of Messenia.

Polybius[4] is the earliest extant author who speaks of 'the rule about landed property, of which no one is allowed to have more, and all the citizens must have an equal share of the civic land'. He cites as his general authorities for the Spartan constitution Plato, Ephorus, Xenophon and Callisthenes. Nothing about land distribution is to be found in Xenophon, the works of Callisthenes are lost, and the only reference in Plato is a statement in the Laws.[5] 'The lawgivers did not incur the greatest of criticisms in arranging some equality of property for them. This happens in many other cities which receive legislation, if one tries to disturb property rights or abolish debts, seeing that equality could not otherwise be created. But every lawgiver who attempts to disturb such rights is resisted by those who say that the existing situation should be left undisturbed, and curse the man who introduces distribution of land and abolition of debts. So that everyone is reduced to impotence. But in this too the Dorians are lucky and

[1] Plut. *Lyc.* 8.   [2] Plut. *Lyc.* 16.   [3] Plut. *Agis*, 8.   [4] VI. 45, 48.   [5] 684de.

without ill will, that the land was distributed without controversy and there were no great or ancient debts.' Plato in fact imagined that the primitive Dorians divided up the land equally after the conquest, and by implication denied any Lycurgan redistribution.

Ephorus' remarks on Crete (he wrote in the middle of the fourth century B.C.) are summarized by Strabo:[1] 'Harmony results when disunity is abolished, which is caused by avarice and luxury. For if everyone lives soberly and simply, there is neither envy nor hatred nor insolence among peers; so they make the boys go into the so-called herds, and adults into the messes, which they call Andreia, so that the poor may share and share alike with the rich.' Of Sparta Polybius[2] says that under the Lycurgan regime 'equality in their possessions and the simplicity and communism of their daily life made their private lives sober and kept the public constitution free from faction'. In a later chapter[3] he writes: 'Lycurgus, it would seem to me, legislated and provided so well towards the mutual harmony of the citizens and towards maintaining the security of Laconia and guarding firmly the freedom of Sparta that his wisdom may be considered superhuman. The equality in estates and the simplicity and community of daily life were bound to make their private lives sober and their common political life free from faction.'

It is clear that Polybius derived his account of Sparta from the same source as that which Strabo used for his account of Crete, that is Ephorus. Moreover, Justin[4] says that Lycurgus 'divided the estates of all among all so that equalized patrimonies should make no one superior to his neighbour', and Justin seems to have derived this part of his history from Ephorus.

Aristotle knew nothing of any system of equal lots of land. His main stricture against Sparta is that the land was concentrated in the hands of a few great owners, mostly women.[5] He criticized the land law. 'He (Lycurgus) made it dishonourable to buy or sell landed property, doing rightly, but he allowed gifts or

---

[1] X. 480.   [2] VI. 45.   [3] VI. 48.   [4] III. iii. 3.   [5] *Pol.* II. ix. 14–6, 1270a.

41

bequests to all who wished.'[1] Yet he was highly interested in systems of maintaining equality of landed property and gives instances from obscure cities, Locris and Leucas, of rules whereby landed property, or at any rate 'the ancient lot' might not be alienated.[2] He knew of no Lycurgan land distribution. He says that according to Tyrtaeus there was a demand for a redistribution of land after the Messenian war;[3] and he surely would have cited the Lycurgan land reform if he had ever heard of it. It would seem, then, that Aristotle, at any rate when he wrote the *Politics*, had heard nothing of a Lycurgan redistribution of land, or of legislation to preserve equality of estates, but that Ephorus knew of the former at any rate. Aristotle may have followed Ephorus in his Constitution of the Lacedaemonians, which was presumably, like the Constitution of Athens, completed after the *Politics*. A certain Heracleides states in his Constitutions: 'It is considered disgraceful for Lacedaemonians to sell land; and it is not even legal for the ancient portion'.[4] Heracleides was probably a Hellenistic writer, and all his extracts about Athens come out of Aristotle's Constitution of Athens. He may therefore have drawn this remark from Aristotle's Constitution of the Lacedaemonians; but he may have used one of the many later monographs on this subject. Plutarch[5] knows of a similar rule, speaking of 'the anciently established portion; it is not legal to sell it'.

In his Life of Agis[6] he wrote: 'not but what the households preserved the number which Lycurgus had fixed by hereditary succession, and father left his lot to his son. . . . But a powerful man, stubborn and harsh by temperament, Epitadeus by name, became ephor, and because he had a quarrel with his son proposed a *rhetra* that it should be legal to donate *inter vivos* or leave by will one's house and lot to whomsoever one wished.' Epitadeus is implied to have lived in the fourth century. This suggests that hitherto a Spartan had only been able to give or bequeath his land if he had no son.

[1] *Pol.* II. ix. 14, 1270a.   [2] *Pol.* II. vii. 6–7, 1266b.   [3] *Pol.* V. vii. 3–4, 1306b–7a.
[4] Arist. *fr.* 611. 12.   [5] *Inst. Lac.* 22.   [6] Plut. *Agis*, 5.

I would maintain, then, that not only the Lycurgan distribution of land in equal lots, but also the inalienable Spartiate allotment is a myth created in the later fourth century. Not but what the primitive Spartan conquerors of Laconia no doubt assigned lots of land, large to the nobles and small and equal to the commoners, and after the conquest of Messenia did the same.

The myth of the Lycurgan land reform would seem, then, to have come into existence about a generation after Leuctra. It was doubtless based on the fact that many Spartiates held or had recently held farms in Laconia and especially in Messenia of approximately equal size, probably going back to the conquest of Messenia, and in Laconia even earlier. The legal rules may have been inferred from the existing or recent customs, whereby Spartiates normally left their land to their sons and did not sell it. This custom was no doubt more stringently observed with old ancestral farms than with recent acquisitions. Hence the alleged distinction between the 'ancient portion' and other land.

XI

THE ORIGINS OF THE PELOPONNESIAN LEAGUE

EARLY in the sixth century the Spartans waged an unsuccessful war against Tegea.[1] They received an oracle: 'You asked me for Arcadia? You asked me for much. I will not give it to you. There are many men who eat acorns in Arcadia who will stop you. But I am not grudging to you. I will give you Tegea to dance upon with the stamping of feet, and a fair plain to measure out with the rod.'

The Spartans accordingly set out with measuring rods and chains, but the chains were captured by the Tegeates, and still hung in Herodotus' day, and in Pausanias'[2] day too, in the temple of Athena Aleia. The Spartans asked for another oracle and were told: 'There is Tegea of Arcadia in the level place where two winds blow beneath mighty necessity and there is blow against blow, and woe lies upon woe. There the life-producing earth holds the son of Agamemnon, whom if thou shalt gather up thou shalt be superior over Tegea.'[3]

Lichas, one of the Benefactors, went as a secret agent to Tegea, and discovered a forge, and the smith showed him a well which he had dug. He had found a tomb seven cubits long, containing a huge corpse. Lichas returned to Sparta and reported. The Spartans then brought a false charge against Lichas and exiled him. He went as an exile to Tegea and there collected the bones and took them to Sparta.[4]

This was a great propaganda stroke. The Spartans now owned the bones of Orestes, the old Achaean king of Sparta before the Dorian invasion, who had undoubted suzerainty over all the Peloponnese.

[1] Herod. I. 66.   [2] VIII. xlvii. 2.   [3] Herod. I. 67.   [4] Herod. I. 68.

A war with Tegea followed under kings Anaxandridas and Ariston, and the Spartans were victorious. They had started the first war, it is plain, with the object of reducing the Tegeates to helots and dividing their fertile plain into allotments. But now they were wiser, and imposed on the Tegeates a status like that of Perioeci. The treaty is preserved by Plutarch:[1] 'to throw the Messenians out of the country and not to make them good'. The last phrase probably means adopt them as citizens. The clause about the Messenians became common form in all Spartan alliances.

According to Herodotus[2] 'the greater part of the Peloponnese was already subdued to them' by the time that Croesus opened diplomatic relations with Sparta. There is no tradition of war with many states. Elis was always friendly, and Mantinea was always the friend of the enemy of Tegea. But all accepted the suzerainty of Sparta.

The Spartans later claimed great credit for overthrowing tyrants. This was accepted history by Thucydides'[3] day: 'And the tyrants of the Athenians and those of the rest of Greece, which had previously been under tyrants for a long period, were most of them, and the last of them except for those in Sicily, overthrown by the Lacedaemonians'. Later authors were more precise. One[4] says: 'Chilon the Laconian, having become ephor, and Anaxandridas, having been appointed general, overthrew tyrannies among the Greeks, in Sicyon Aeschines and at Athens Hippias the son of Peisistratus'. This sounds very good, for Chilon was by tradition ephor in 556[5] and therefore contemporary with King Anaxandridas.[l] But of the tyrants cited Hippias is impossible; he was expelled in 510.[m] Aeschines of Sicyon may well be right; his fall could date to the mid sixth century.[n] Plutarch in a youthful diatribe de Malignitate Herodoti[6] puts among the tyrants expelled by Sparta the Cypselids at Corinth and at Ambracia, Lygdamis of Naxos, Aeschines of Sicyon, Symmachus of

[1] *Graec. Quaest.* 5.   [2] I. 68.   [3] I. 28.
[4] *P. Ryl.* 18.   [5] Diog. Laert. I. 68.   [6] Ch. 21, *Mor.* 859d.

Thasos, Aules of Phocis, Aristogenes of Miletus and Angelus and Aristomedes in Thessaly. The Corinthian tradition recorded by Herodotus[1] and Ephorus[2] knows nothing of a Spartan expulsion of the Cypselids, and Aristotle's[3] account of Ambracia omits Sparta. Lygdamis of Naxos may have been expelled by the Spartans, but Herodotus does not say so; he would have been expelled about the same time as Hippias of Athens. All the others except Aeschines are unknown.

By the middle of the sixth century Sparta was a world power. She was wooed by King Croesus[4] and utterly failed him when Cyrus the Persian overthrew him. Their excuse was that at the critical moment they were involved in a war with Argos, from which they conquered Thyreatis or Cynuria, the strip of coast east of Mount Parnon running down from Thyrea to Cape Malea and including the island of Cythera.° Finally the Argives demanded that the question be settled by a battle of 300 champions on each side. Herodotus[5] tells the picturesque story how ultimately two Argives and one Spartiate survived, when the two Argives walked off the field as victors, but the Spartiate erected a trophy. There followed a general engagement in which the Argives lost heavily. The population of Thyreatis were treated as Perioeci.

King Amasis of Egypt sent them a magnificent breastplate of linen,[6] and they did nothing for him. The Ionians appealed to Sparta to help them against Cyrus, and 'they sent men in a penteconter. And when they arrived at Phocaea they sent to Sardis the most distinguished among them, whose name was Lacrines, to announce to Cyrus the decision of the Spartans, that he should ravage no city of the land of Hellas, since they would not overlook it. And when the herald said this it is reported that Cyrus asked those Hellenes who were present, who were the

---

[1] V. 92; as the Corinthians are rebuking the Spartans for supporting tyranny at Athens, it would have been most appropriate for them to recall their former expulsion of the Corinthian tyrants.
[2] *FGH.* 90, F60.   [3] Arist. *Pol.* V. iv. 9, 1303a, V. x. 16, 1311ab.
[4] Herod. I. 69–70.   [5] Herod. I. 82.   [6] Herod. III. 47.

46

Lacedaemonians and how many in number that they should speak to him thus.'[1]

The next expedition of the Spartans was more serious. It took place during Cambyses' invasion of Egypt (525). It was undertaken in conjunction with the Corinthians against Polycrates, tyrant of Samos. Both attackers had many grievances. The Spartans wished to avenge the loss at sea of the famous linen corslet which Amasis had sent them, and also of the mixing bowl which the Spartans had sent to Croesus.[2] They had also received an appeal from exiled Samian nobles, who subsequently settled in Crete.[3] These exiles had a claim on the Spartan government in that their ancestors had helped Sparta during the second Messenian war.[4] The Corinthian grievance was that in a previous generation the Samians had given sanctuary to 300 noble Corcyraean boys whom Periander, tyrant of Corinth, was sending to Alyattes, king of Lydia, to be castrated.[5]

The Spartans effected a landing and besieged the town of Samos. Their attempts to storm the city were beaten back and after a forty days, siege they withdrew in good order.[6]

---

[1] Herod. I. 152-3. [2] Herod. I. 70, III. 47. [3] Herod. III. 44.
[4] Herod. III. 47. [5] Herod. III. 48. [6] Herod. III. 54-6.

XII

CLEOMENES I

WE now come to the reign of one of the greatest of the
Spartan kings, Cleomenes. 'His father Anaxandridas had
married his own sister's daughter and though she was pleasing to
him they had no sons. And when this was so, the ephors called
on him and said: "If you have no forethought for yourself, we
cannot allow this, that the race of Eurysthenes should become
extinct. The wife that you have, since she is barren, cast her out, and
marry another. And if you do this you will please the Spartiates."
And he answered and said that he would do neither of these
things, and in their counsel they were advising him badly, to
send away the wife he had, who was without fault to himself,
and bring in another; and that he would not obey them. At this
the ephors and the elders took counsel and made the following
proposition to Anaxandridas. "Since we can see that you cling
to the wife that you have, yet do this and do not resist these
men, lest the Spartiates make some untoward decision about you.
We do not ask you for the expulsion of the wife which you have,
but do you provide for her all that you now provide and introduce another wife in addition to have children." And when they
said this Anaxandridas agreed, and after this he had two wives
and maintained two hearths, acting by no means in the Spartiate
fashion. And after a short while the wife that came in afterwards
bore Cleomenes. And she displayed him to the Spartiates as the
heir apparent. And the former wife, who had formerly been
barren, then conceived. . . . And when she had borne Dorieus,
she immediately had Leonidas and shortly after that she had
Cleombrotus; and some say that Leonidas and Cleombrotus were
twins. But the mother of Cleomenes, the second wife, who was

the daugher of Prinetades, son of Demarmenus, never had a second child.'[1]

Actually it is not certain that Dorieus was the eldest son, as he left a son, Euryanax, who survived till 479, but did not become king, as he would have done by the law of primogeniture.[2] Dorieus himself, furious at being passed over when Cleomenes succeeded, led a colony to Africa, taking a group of Spartiates. But he obtained no oracle from Delphi. Guided by some Therans he shipped his men to Cinyps in Libya. After three years he was expelled by the Macae, the Libyans and the Carthaginians, and returned to the Peloponnese. He was advised according to ancient oracles to settle Heraclea in Sicily, as all the land of Eryx belonged to the Heraclids. He then obtained a favourable reply from Delphi, but on the way stopped in Italy to assist Croton against Sybaris. After this Dorieus and his four fellow founders went to Sicily and were defeated by the Phoenicians and Segestans and killed.[3]

As Cleomenes reigned over twenty years his half-brothers naturally resented the intruder, and as he left no male heirs his name was not unnaturally blackened. His first recorded act was in 519 B.C.[4P] He must have been operating in the Megarid, perhaps bringing Megara under Spartan suzerainty, when the Plataeans, being at odds with the Thebans, appealed to him. Cleomenes was too wily to incur the enmity of Thebes, and advised the Plataeans to appeal to Athens, then under the tyrant Hippias, who had studiously cultivated friendly relations with all the great powers, Sparta, Argos, Thebes and Thessaly.[5]

Cleomenes next received an appeal from Samos. When Polycrates was killed by the Persian satrap Oroetes, Maeandrius, son of Maeandrius, his regent, 'wished to be the justest of men, but it did not come off'. He abdicated, reserving for himself only six talents and the hereditary priesthood of Zeus of Liberty. The

---

[1] Herod. V. 39–41.   [2] Herod. IX. 10.   [3] Herod. V. 42–6.
[4] Thuc. III. 68.   [5] Herod. VI. 108.

citizens insultingly rejected the offer and the Persians occupied the island.[1]

Maeandrius sailed to Sparta and landed with large numbers of gold and silver drinking vessels. He promised Cleomenes as many as he liked, but the king 'went to the ephors and said it was better for Sparta that the Samian stranger should be removed from the Peloponnese, lest he should persuade himself or any other of the Spartiates to be evil, and they obeyed and banished Maeandrius'. Cleomenes had no intention of getting involved in hostilities with Persia.[2]

The next embassy was from the Scythians, who after Darius had invaded their country in 514 proposed a gigantic combined operation, whereby they were to invade Media via the Caucasus and the Spartans to land at Ephesus for the same objective. The only result was that Cleomenes took to drink.[3]

Next follow his complicated dealings with Athens. The exiled Alcmaeonids, having secured control of Delphi, got the Pythia to give repeated oracles to Sparta to free Athens. The Spartans first sent Anchimolius with a seaborne expedition.[4] He is the first known holder of the office of admiral or navarch; the navarch had the same absolute authority over the fleet as the king had over the army,[5] but the office was annual and could not be held by the same person twice.[6] Anchimolius was repulsed, and the Spartans then sent Cleomenes with a proper army. He besieged the Acropolis and the Peisistratidae withdrew under safe conduct. There then followed a political struggle between Isagoras, who wished to establish an aristocracy, and Cleisthenes the Alcmaeonid, who appealed to the people. Isagoras was beaten in the contest, and appealed to Cleomenes. He sent a herald to Athens to order the expulsion of the 'accursed' Alcmaeonidae.[7]

Cleomenes now appeared with a small army to enforce the order and seized the Acropolis. It was on this occasion, when the priestess of Athena refused him entry to her temple because he

---

[1] Herod. III. 142-7.　　[2] Herod. III. 148.　　[3] Herod. VI. 84.　　[4] Herod. V. 63.
[5] Arist. *Pol.* II. ix. 33, 1271a.　　[6] Xen. *Hell.* II. i. 7; Plut. *Lys.* 7.　　[7] Herod. V. 63-5, 70.

was a Dorian, that Cleomenes made his famous claim, 'Lady, I am not a Dorian but an Achaean'. Which was true, since he was a Heraclid. The Athenian council rallied the people and besieged the Acropolis for two days, after which the Spartans marched out under safe conduct.[1]

Upon this Cleomenes 'summoned an army, from all the Peloponnese, not telling them their objective', intending to install Isagoras as tyrant. The Peloponnesian army invaded Eleusis, the Thebans simultaneously seized Oenoe and Hysiae, and the Chalcidians ravaged the eastern coast of Attica. At this point the Corinthian contingent refused to fight, and Demaratus, the other king, supported them. The expedition broke up, the Thebans and Chalcidians were separately defeated by Athens.[2]

This incident produced, as we have seen, an important constitutional change in Sparta. 'A law was passed that it should be unlawful for both kings to be present when the army marched out',[3] which meant effectively that henceforth the kings could not wage war on their own initiative. This change does not seem to have affected Cleomenes' personal ascendancy in Sparta.

The Spartans then sent for Hippias, who had taken refuge in Persia, and summoned a congress of all their allies. The Corinthians spoke vigorously against tyranny, and the expedition was dropped.[4] Cleomenes is not mentioned in connection with this move, but it seems likely that he was behind it, since it falls into line with his previous policy of reducing the recalcitrant Athenians to obedience by putting them under a tyrant who would be a puppet of Sparta. This debate marks the development of the Spartan hegemony into the Peloponnesian League. Hitherto it would seem the allies had been bound to obey the Spartan kings without question and sent their contingents on demand. Henceforth they were consulted when Sparta wished to go to war. It is also, incidentally, the first of many occasions when the Corinthians rocked the boat.

[1] Herod. V. 72.   [2] Herod. V. 74–7.   [3] Herod. V. 75.   [4] Herod. V. 91 ff.

We know a good deal about the detailed constitution of the League in later times. The members were all supposed to be autonomous allies of Sparta.[1] In time of peace they were entitled to go to war with one another,[2] but if attacked by an outside power they could appeal for aid to Sparta.[3] If the Spartan assembly decided that there was a *casus belli*, a meeting of delegates from all members was held.[4] All cities great and small had one vote, and the vote of the majority decided the issue. Internal wars between members had then to be suspended,[5] and the Spartans levied the federal army, each city contributing two-thirds of its fighting strength,[6] and the city in whose territory the army was to meet its full strength.[7] A Spartan king took command, and Spartan officers, styled *xenagi*, levied the contingents of the cities.[8] Peace was made by a majority vote of the allies, but there was an escape clause, 'unless there be an impediment of gods or heroes'.[9] The Spartans were also entitled to aid from their allies if the Helots revolted. This is stated in the treaty with Athens of 421,[10] and in the Messenian revolt of 465 the Spartans were assisted by the Athenians,[11] the Plataeans,[12] the Aeginetans,[13] and the Mantineans.[14]

The Ionian cities subject to Persia now (499) decided to revolt and sent an envoy to Sparta, Aristagoras, ex-tyrant of Miletus. He carried with him a map of the world in bronze, and displayed it to King Cleomenes, suggesting exciting prospects of conquest and booty. Cleomenes asked him how far it was from the Ionian coast to the great king's capital, and Aristagoras airily replied, 'Three months'. Cleomenes replied, 'Stranger of Miletus, remove yourself from Sparta before the setting of the sun; for you speak no well-spoken words to the Lacedaemonians, wishing to lead them three months' journey from the sea'. Aristagoras presented

[1] Thuc. V. 77, 79.   [2] Thuc. IV. 134, V. 29, 31; Xen. *Hell.* V. iv. 36–7.
[3] Thuc. V. 77.   [4] Thuc. I. 125.
[5] Thuc. V. 29, 31; Xen. *Hell.* V. iv. 36–7.   [6] Thuc. II. 10.   [7] Thuc. V. 57.
[8] Thuc. II. 75; Xen. *Hell.* III. v. 7, V. i. 33, ii. 7, VII. ii. 3.   [9] Thuc. V. 30.
[10] Thuc. V. 23.   [11] Thuc. I. 102.   [12] Thuc. III. 54.   [13] Thuc. II. 27.
[14] Xen. *Hell.* V. ii. 3.

himself as a suppliant at Cleomenes' house, and offered ten talents. He went up to fifty talents. And then little Gorgo, Cleomenes' daughter, said: 'Father, the stranger will corrupt you unless you get up and go away'.[1]

Aristagoras went on to Athens, and finding it easier to fool 30,000 Athenians than King Cleomenes, persuaded them to send 20 ships to Ionia.[2] He also tried Argos, but an embassy to Delphi by the Argives produced frightful denunciations of woe upon both Miletus and Argos.[3]

It is probable that a 50-years truce between Sparta and Argos ran out in 496. Cleomenes seized his opportunity.[q] Leading a purely Lacedaemonian force he sacrificed at the river Erasinus, the boundary of Spartan and Argive territory. The omens were unfavourable and Cleomenes said that he admired the Erasinus for not betraying his fellow citizens but that the Argives would rue it none the less. He marched his force to Thyrea and thence shipped it to Tiryns and Nauplia, where he landed unopposed. The Argive generals decided to follow the Spartan heralds' signals, and Cleomenes observing this ordered the heralds to sound for breakfast, and this should be the signal for the advance.[4]

The Spartans slaughtered vast numbers of Argives at Sepeia and penned many more in a sacred grove. These Cleomenes lured out by pretending that he had received their ransoms, and slaughtered them in cold blood. When the Argives spotted what was happening he fired the grove. Six thousand Argives were killed.[5] None the less his enemies denounced him to the ephors for having been bribed into sparing the city of Argos. He was acquitted.[6]

Not long after this the great King Darius sent heralds to all the cities of Greece, demanding earth and water. The Athenians and Spartans threw the heralds into a pit and a well, telling them to find earth and water there, but most of the other Greek cities, including Aegina, yielded.[7] Now Aegina had for some time

[1] Herod. V. 49 ff.   [2] Herod. V. 97.   [3] Herod. VI. 19, 77   [4] Herod. VI. 76–8.
[5] Herod. VII. 148.   [6] Herod. VI. 78–82.   [7] Herod. VII. 48–9, 133.

been waging a war 'without heralds' upon Athens, and the Athenians were not unnaturally fearful that they might abet the Persian attack on their city. They appealed to Cleomenes, who promptly crossed to Aegina and tried to arrest the most distinguished Aeginetans. He was resisted by Crius, the son of Polycritus, who said, 'He would arrest any of the Aeginetans at his peril; for he was acting in this without the commonwealth of the Spartans, having been bought by the Athenians. For if he had come with the other king he could have made his arrests.' This he said under the prompting of Cleomenes' colleague Demaratus.[1]

Events now moved very fast. Cleomenes decided to get rid of Demaratus. His father Ariston had had two wives, who were both barren, and finally married a third, the beautiful wife of his greatest friend. Before ten months were up she bore him Demaratus. When the news was brought to Ariston, sitting with the ephors, he counted up the months on his fingers and said: 'He could not be mine'. Cleomenes accordingly approached Leotychidas, who stood next in the line of succession, and had a feud with Demaratus, and extracted from him an undertaking that he would support Cleomenes against the Aeginetans. Leotychidas denounced Demaratus as a bastard, producing the ephors of the day of his birth as witnesses. The Spartans decided to consult Delphi, and Cleomenes secured the appropriate response.[2]

Cleomenes and Leotychidas went to Aegina, and the Aeginetans 'when both the kings came to them, no longer felt justified in resisting'. The kings picked out ten of the most distinguished Aeginetans, including Crius, and sent them to Attica as hostages. It is interesting to note how even the allied cities of Sparta still acknowledged the absolute power of the two kings acting in concert.[3]

Very soon after this Cleomenes' plot against Demaratus leaked out, and he fled the country. When Cleomenes was out of the

[1] Herod. VI. 50.   [2] Herod. VI. 61–6.   [3] Herod. VI. 73.

54

way the Aeginetans denounced Leotychidas about their hostages. The Spartans brought Leotychidas to trial, and decided that he should be surrendered to the Aeginetans. The Aeginetans were afraid to accept this offer, but begged Leotychidas to demand the return of their hostages from Athens. The Athenians, however, refused to surrender them.[1]

Cleomenes fled to Thessaly. From there he moved into Arcadia, and 'tried to raise the Arcadians against Sparta, and to impose on them various oaths that they would follow him wherever he led them'. Finally he was eager that the leaders of the Arcadians should swear by the waters of the Styx at the city of Nonacris. The Spartans in alarm received him back as king, but he went mad, hitting every Spartiate he met on the face with his sceptre. His relatives chained him in the stocks, but he bullied his Helot guard into giving him a knife and sliced himself in pieces.[2] This at any rate was the official story.

So died one of the greatest of the Spartan kings. He crushed Argos for a generation, and extended Spartan suzerainty north of the Isthmus. But his interests were confined to Sparta and he ignored the approaching Persian peril. He abandoned Samos and the Ionians to the Persians. He was willing, it seems, to install the pro-Persian Hippias in Athens. Even his intervention against Aegina was probably designed primarily to bring Athens under Spartan hegemony.

[1] Herod. VI. 85–6.   [2] Herod. VI. 74–5.

XIII

THE PERSIAN WARS

WHEN the Persians landed at Marathon the Athenians sent a runner, Philippides, to Sparta. He arrived at Sparta in two days, and gave his message:[1]

'O Lacedaemonians, the Athenians beg you to help them and not to sit by while the most ancient city amongst the Hellenes falls into slavery at the hands of barbarian men; for now Eretria has been enslaved and Hellas is the poorer by a famous city'.

The Spartans agreed, but as it was the ninth of the month said that they could not march until the full moon.[2] Plato thought this excuse inadequate and invented a third Messenian war to account for Spartan reluctance.[3 1] However, at the full moon 2,000 Spartans marched in three days to Athens, and were shown the piles of Persian dead.[4]

The defence of Greece against Xerxes was by unanimous consent led by Sparta. The policy of the confederation of the Hellenes was decided by a council of delegates over which the Spartans presided, and the Spartan regent or king commanded both the land and sea forces. When the Argives offered to join the confederacy if they could share the command they were refused.[5] The Athenians, though they provided the bulk of the allied fleet, never claimed the naval command.[6]

Spartan strategy was excessively cautious. There may have been adequate strategical and political reasons for abandoning the Pass of Tempe and thus throwing all the Thessalians into Persian hands. Thermopylae should, however, have been more

[1] Herod. VI. 105–6. [2] Herod. VI. 106. [3] *Laws*, 692d, 698e.
[4] Herod. VI. 120. [5] Herod. VII. 148–9. [6] Herod. VII. 161.

firmly held. King Leonidas and his 300 Spartiates covered themselves with glory. C'était magnifique, mais ce n'était pas la guerre. A few thousand Spartans on the Anopaea Pass, instead of the unreliable Phocians, could have made Thermopylae impregnable.

The Spartans then retired to the isthmus of Corinth, which they entrenched. It was only by a trick that Themistocles got the Greek fleet to stay in the bay of Salamis, and thus achieved the destruction of the Persian fleet. Even after this, when the Persian army had been reduced to a reasonable size, it was only by a threat of migration to the west that the Athenians forced the Spartans to advance into Boeotia. But at the battle of Plataea the Spartan contingent, 5,000 strong with 5,000 Perioeci, played the decisive role.

King Leotychidas now took courage and advanced with the fleet across the Aegean and won the great battle of Mycale. He received the cities of Lesbos, Chios and Samos into the Hellenic alliance, but would do nothing for the mainland Ionians. He proposed that they should migrate *en masse* to lands annexed from the Medizing communities of Greece.[1] When the summer closed he, with the other allied contingents, left the Athenians to besiege and win Sestos, the key city of the Hellespont.[2]

Next year Pausanias, son of Cleombrotus, regent for Pleistarchus, the infant son of Leonidas, took command of the fleet. He acted with vigour, capturing Byzantium and supporting the revolt of the Cypriot cities. But his success went to his head. He adopted the dress and manners of a Persian satrap, treated the allies with haughty disdain, and entered into a treasonable correspondence with the Great King. The ephors recalled him but too late. The Ionians transferred their allegiance to Athens and the Delian League was born. Dorcis, who was sent out as navarch next year (478), found himself helpless and returned.[3]

Pausanias was tried at Sparta but acquitted, and sailed in 478 in a private ship to Byzantium. There he carried on his negotiations with Xerxes, and adopted an even more oriental display of

[1] Herod. IX. 106.   [2] Herod. IX. 114.   [3] Thuc. I. 94–5.

57

royalty. He was expelled from Byzantium by the Athenians, and went to Colonae in the Troad. The ephors sent a herald with a coded message that he was to follow the herald or the Spartiates would declare war on him. Pausanias returned to Sparta and was imprisoned by the ephors, was released and offered to stand his trial. The ephors had no clear evidence of treason, but it was feared that Pausanias might raise the Helots by promising them freedom and citizenship. Eventually a man of Argilus, his go-between to Persia, betrayed him. The go-between took sanctuary on Taenarum, and an interview was staged between him and Pausanias, with the ephors listening in. The ephors now ordered the arrest, but one of them warned Pausanias, who took refuge in the temple of Athena Chalcioecus. The ephors starved him out.[1]

[1] Thuc. I. 128–34.

XIV

THE PENTEKONTAETEIA

A T about the same time the other king Leotychidas led a Spartan army to Thessaly to punish the Medizing cities. Large quantities of silver were found in his pouch, and he was tried and exiled. He took refuge in Tegea.[1]

If the Spartan regent succumbed to megalomania and the king to bribes, the home authorities were as disastrously inept. They proposed that the cities north of the isthmus of Corinth should not rebuild their walls, in case they should serve as strongholds for the Persians in a second invasion. By a famous ruse Themistocles defeated this move. Having arranged that the walls of Athens should be forthwith rebuilt, he went as envoy to Sparta, and spun out negotiations until they were sufficiently high to resist attack.[2]

It is stated by Thucydides that when the Ionians transferred their allegiance to Athens, 'the Lacedaemonians sent out no more commanders (after Dorcis), fearing that those whom they sent should deteriorate, as they had observed in the case of Pausanias, and wishing to be freed from the Persian war and thinking that the Athenians were adequate leaders and convenient for themselves at the present juncture'.[3]

This was no doubt the view of the older and more sober Spartiates, but the decision was not made without a profound internal struggle in Sparta. It is recorded by Diodorus,[4] that is Ephorus, under a wrong year (475). A meeting of the *gerusia* was held, and the question of war with Athens was debated. A meeting of the assembly was also held and a majority, including all the younger men, were for war. The *gerusia* had, however,

---

[1] Herod. VI. 72.   [2] Thuc. I. 90–3.   [3] Thuc. I. 95.   [4] XI. 50.

not voted, and one of its members, Hetoemaridas, a Heraclid of great distinction, persuaded both it and the people to vote against the motion.

The Spartans had, however, no opportunity for revenge. Their prestige had collapsed utterly, and their position in the Peloponnesian homeland was challenged. All we know of these wars is that fact that Tisamenus of Elis took the auspices at five Spartan victories, Plataea, Tegea, against the Tegeates and Argives, Dipaea, against all the Arcadians except the Mantineans, Ithome, against the Messenians, and Tanagra, against the Athenians and Argives.[1] It was about this time (between his ostracism in 471 and his exile in 465)[5] that Themistocles was living at Argos and travelling about the rest of the Peloponnese,[2] and that the villages of Elis were amalgamated into a city,[3] and probably too that the four villages of Mantinea also became a city.[4] Both these cities probably now adopted the democratic constitutions which they later had.[5] About Elis and Mantinea the Spartans could do nothing, little though they liked democracy after their experience of Athens, as they were loyal allies; nor could they interfere with Argos which, though defeated, was unsubdued. If the other Arcadian cities had liberalized their constitutions, they were compelled to revert to oligarchy.

In 465 the Thasians, allies of Athens but at war with her, appealed to Sparta for aid. The ephors apparently belonged in this year to the war party, and seeing that Spartan hands were at last free, secretly promised to invade Attica.[6] This treacherous act—for Athens was an ally of Sparta—was frustrated by the great earthquake.[t]

This disaster apparently killed hundreds if not thousands of Spartiates. Diodorus[7] declares that only five houses remained standing in the town, and puts the total casualties at 20,000. The

[1] Herod. IX. 35.   [2] Thuc. I. 135.
[3] Diod. XI. 54, under the year 471; Strabo, VIII. 336.
[4] Strabo, VIII. 337, Xen. Hell. V. ii. 7. Strabo says five villages, but Xenophon's four is more likely to be right.
[5] Thuc. V. 29, Xen. Hell. III. ii. 27 ff.   [6] Thuc. I. 101.   [7] XI. 63.

mortality was particularly heavy among the Spartan boys between 13 and 18, who were crushed by the collapse of their gymnasium.[1]

There followed the third Messenian war, in which not only the Messenian helots, but two Messenian Perioecic towns, Thuria and Aethaea, and some Laconian Helots joined.[2] The war soon resolved itself into a siege of Ithome, but the Spartans were very hard pressed, and called for and received aid not only from their Peloponnesian allies (Mantinea and Aegina are mentioned) but also from their allies in the Hellenic alliance, Plataea and finally Athens. In 461 the Athenians sent 4,000 hoplites under Cimon,[3] but 'the Lacedaemonians when the place was not captured, fearing the daring and revolutionary spirit of the Athenians, and thinking that as foreigners they might, if they stayed on, be won over by the inhabitants of Ithome and make a revolution, dismissed them alone of their allies'.[4]

It must have been after the great earthquake that Sparta reorganized its army into the form which it possessed at the time of the battle of Mantinea and in Xenophon's day.[u] The main point of the reform was that all Lacedaemonians, Spartiates and Perioeci, were brigaded together; the Spartans did not dare to uncover their nakedness. This is nowhere stated, but the evidence is unequivocal. In many descriptions of the Spartan army *morae* or *lochoi* of Lacedaemonians are mentioned, but never of Spartiates or Perioeci. For the occupation of Pylos 420 men were taken by lot from all the *lochoi*; the survivors numbered about 120 Spartiates and about 170 others.[5] Spartiates were brigaded without regard to their obe or their family. Amyclaeans were to be found throughout the whole army.[6] Fathers, sons and brothers were to be found in different *morae*.[7] The precise organization is not altogether clear. Besides the Sciritae (600 strong), who were still brigaded separately on the left wing, there were six *morae*, commanded by polemarchs; each *mora* was divided into four

---

[1] Plut. *Cimon*, 16. [2] Thuc. I. 101. [3] Aristoph. *Lysistrata*, 1143–4. See note cc.
[4] Thuc. I. 102. [5] Thuc. IV. 8, 38. [6] Xen. *Hell*. IV. v. 11. [7] Ib. IV. v. 10.

lochoi, commanded by *lochagoi*, and each *lochos* into two *pente-costyes* under *pentecosteres* and each *pentecostys* into two *enomotiae* under enomotiarchs. The strength of the *enomotia* varied according to the number of age classes called up; on one occasion it numbered 36 men. This yields a total of 3,456. This is Xenophon's arrangement.[1] Thucydides[2] conflates the *morae* with the *lochoi*, producing six *lochoi*, each with four *pentecostyes*, each with four *enomotiae*. On this occasion the *enomotia* numbered 32, so that the total comes to 3,072. Both authors are fairly certainly mistaken, for in the early fourth century the Lacedaemonian levy was 6,000.[3] Xenophon should have said four *enomotiae* to a *pentecostys*. The figure is a big drop from the 10,000 mustered for Plataea.

In their military arrangements the Spartans did not keep to Lycurgus. They were thoroughly up to date. They wore uniform—a scarlet coat, bronze shield and long hair.[4] They marched to the piper.[5] They had a wagon train to carry their heavy equipment.[6] They had a commissariat system. Xenophon describes how a *mora* was bivouacking near Corinth, 'and none of those bringing food to the *mora* had carried fire', but 'Agesilaus sent not less than ten men carrying fire in pots'.[7] Above all, they had a chain of command and could execute complicated manœuvres, forming to flank or reversing on the battlefield without confusion. Xenophon[8] waxes lyrical in describing their parade ground drill, and Thucydides[9] describes the chain of command with awe. The king 'himself gives the necessary orders to the polemarchs, and they to the *lochagoi*, and they to the *penteconteres*, and they to the enomotarchs, and they to the *enomotia*. And messages, if anything is required, go by the same channel and arrive quickly. Practically all the Lacedaemonian army are commanders of commanders.'

[1] *Resp. Lac.* xi. 4, *Hell.* VI. iv. 12.   [2] V. 68, cf. 71.   [3] Xen. *Hell.* IV. ii. 16.
[4] Xen. *Resp. Lac.* xi. 3.   [5] Thuc. V. 70.   [6] Xen. *Resp. Lac.* xi. 2.
[7] Xen. *Hell.* IV. v. 4.   [8] *Resp. Lac.* xi. 6 ff.   [9] V. 66.

The Spartans at this date had no cavalry. There was, it is true, a body of '300 picked Spartiates who are called cavalry';[1] they were chosen by three commanders, called *hippagretae*, who were themselves nominated by the ephors.[2] They were in fact not cavalry, but an infantry bodyguard for the king.[3] It was not until 424 that the Spartans raised a cavalry force, 400 strong,[4] later increased to 600.[5] It was according to Xenophon[6] a very inefficient force. The horses were maintained by the richest citizens, but they did not ride them. When a levy was proclaimed the men called up as troopers took the horses and the arms allocated to them; but service in the cavalry was not considered as honourable and the troopers were the physically feeblest and the least ambitious men.

The result of the insulting dismissal of the Athenian contingent was war with Athens. The Athenians denounced their old alliance with Sparta against the Persians, and formed alliances with Argos and Thessaly.[7] The war began with the defection of Megara from the Peloponnesian League,[8] which brought in Corinth, Epidaurus, and Aegina, which the Athenians besieged.[9] The Spartans were at first helpless, but at length in 457 they sent a force of 1,500 Lacedaemonians and 10,000 allies, professedly to succour Doris against the Phocians. The leader of this force was Nicomedes, the son of Cleombrotus, regent for Pleistoanax, the son of Pausanias. Evidently Archidamus, the grandson of Leotychidas, the hero of the third Messenian war,[10] refused to serve. The huge army was shipped across the gulf of Corinth, duly rescued Doris, and moved into Boeotia, where it apparently re-asserted Spartan supremacy under the leadership of Thebes. The Athenians marched out in full force, with 1,000 Argives and other allied contingents, 14,000 in all, and a great battle was fought at Tanagra. It was a costly draw. The Spartans, disappointed of their hope of seizing Athens by the treachery of the oligarchic party, marched

[1] Herod. VIII. 124, cf. I. 67.   [2] Xen. *Resp. Lac.* iv. 3.
[3] Thuc. V. 72; Strabo, X, 481–2.   [4] Thuc. IV. 55.
[5] Xen. *Hell.* IV. ii. 16.   [6] *Hell.* VI. iv. 11.   [7] Thuc. I. 102.
[8] Thuc. I. 103.   [9] Thuc. I. 105.   [10] Plut. *Cimon*, 16, Diod. XI. 63.

quietly home. The Athenians let them pass through the mountain track of Geraneia, withdrawing their garrisons. But they immediately defeated the Boeotians at Oenophyta and brought them into their alliance together with the Phocians and Opuntian Locrians. Aegina fell in the same year.[1]

Next year the Great King sent an agent, Megabazus, to the Spartans, hoping to persude them to invade Attica—he wished to divert Athens from Egypt—but though the Spartans—or some Spartans—accepted a great deal of money from Megabazus they took no action.[2] Three years later in 451 the Spartans and Athenians made a five-year truce.[3] Two or three years after this Sparta rejected an olive branch proferred by Athens. The Athenians proposed that a Panhellenic congress should be held to settle all the outstanding questions from the Persian wars, the performance of the sacrifices then vowed to the gods, the restoration of the temples destroyed by the Persians and finally the freedom of the seas. Invitations were issued to all Greek states, to the Ionians and Dorians in Asia and the islands, to the cities of Hellespont and Thrace, to the Boeotians, Phocians, Peloponnesians, Locrians, Acarnanians and Ambraciots, and to Euboea, the Oetaeans, Achaeans and Thessalians. The agenda was, it is true, more interesting to Athens than to Sparta. The only temples which the Persians had burnt down were those of Athens, and the freedom of the seas could only be maintained by the Delian League (these items were in effect requests for Panhellenic sanction for spending the accumulated fund formerly at Delos, now at Athens, on rebuilding the Athenian temples, and for keeping the Delian League in being, when its *raison d'être* had been removed by the Peace of Callias). Nevertheless, Pericles' gesture was a liberal one, and if Sparta had responded something like a general confederation of Hellas might have emerged. But the Spartans refused the invitation.[4]

As soon as the five-years truce lapsed the Spartans took advantage of a revolt of the Euboeans and the Megarians to invade

[1] Thuc. I. 107–8.   [2] Thuc. I. 109.   [3] Thuc. I. 112.   [4] Plut. *Pericles*, 17.

64

Attica. The army was led by the young king Pleistoanax, son of Pausanias. He retreated without effecting anything, and not long afterwards the Thirty Years Peace was signed.[1]

By this famous treaty Athens renounced not only her claims to Boeotia and Megara, but Nisaea and Pegae, the two Megarian ports, which she still held, and also Troezen and Achaea, which she had recently won. Sparta on the other hand abandoned Aegina, only stipulating that the Aeginetans should be autonomous members of the Delian League.[2] Neutral states were allowed to join either confederacy.[3] Argos, which had in 451 pulled out of the Athenian alliance and made a Thirty Years Truce with Sparta,[4] was allowed to make a separate treaty with Athens.[5] There was also a clause that any disputes should be submitted to arbitration.[6]

The whole incident is rather mysterious and suggests a sharp division of sentiment at Sparta. It is significant that once again the Spartans did not assign the command to Archidamus, but to Pleistoanax, who was so young that the ephors had to appoint advisers to guide him.[7] Evidently Archidamus disapproved of the invasion and either refused to serve or was distrusted by the war party. Pleistoanax's withdrawal is also very strange. He and his principal adviser, Cleandridas, were later accused of having accepted bribes from Pericles, but, even if they did, they would hardly have acted as they did unless they hoped to justify their action to the Spartan government. It must be presumed that Pericles offered them the terms later embodied in the Thirty Years Peace and that they thought them satisfactory. The *gerusia* evidently did not; for Pleistoanax was heavily fined and had to go into exile and Cleandridas also fled the country and was condemned to death in absence.[8] The assembly, however, ratified the Thirty Years Peace, on the advice, one may suspect, of Archidamus.

[1] Thuc. I. 114–15.   [2] Thuc. I. 67, 139–40.   [3] Thuc. I. 35, 40.
[4] Thuc. V. 14, 28.   [5] Paus. V. xxiii, 4.   [6] Thuc. I. 78, 140, 144–5.
[7] Plut. *Pericles*, 22, *Nicias*, 28.
[8] Plut. *Pericles*, 22, schol. on Aristophanes, *Clouds*, 859. Suidas, s.v. λέον.

In 440 Samos rebelled from Athens and asked for Spartan aid. The Corinthians a few years later recalled to the Athenians the good turn that they had done them with regard to the Samians, 'the fact that owing to us the Peloponnesians did not assist them' . . . 'for when the Samians revolted we did not cast our vote against you, when the other Peloponnesians were divided in their vote as to whether they ought to help, but spoke out boldly'.[1] The constitution of the Peloponnesian League was such that the congress of allies never debated a declaration of war until and unless Sparta had decided for war. So this means that the Spartans decided upon a flagrant breach of the Thirty Years Peace only six years after its signature.

We now come to the complicated train of events which led to the Peloponnesian war. It all began with a quarrel between Corinth and her ungrateful colony Corcyra.[2] Corcyra, hard pressed, appealed to Athens.[3] It was perfectly legal for Athens to form an alliance with Corcyra, a neutral, but it was hardly tactful, and would certainly lead to war with Corinth. On the other hand Corcyra possessed the second navy in Greece, and to allow it to fall into the hands of Corinth was too great a risk, when Sparta was obviously spoiling for war. The Athenians did their best by making a strictly defensive alliance with Corcyra[4] and limiting their intervention to saving the Corcyraean fleet.[5] But they had baulked the Corinthians of their revenge.

Athens next tried to discipline Potidaea, a Corinthian colony which was a member of the Delian League, fearing that it would revolt.[6] The Spartan authorities, despite the Thirty Years Peace, promised to invade Attica if the Potidaeans revolted,[7] and Corinth gave them military support.[8] Finally, taking advantage of a technical sacrilege of the Megarians, Athens excluded the Megarians from the Athenian market and all the ports of the Delian League.[9]

[1] Thuc. I. 40, 41.   [2] Thuc. I. 24 ff.   [3] Thuc. I. 31 ff.
[4] Thuc. I. 44.   [5] Thuc. I. 45 ff.   [6] Thuc. I. 56 ff.
[7] Thuc. I. 58, 71.   [8] Thuc. I. 60 ff.   [9] Thuc. I. 67

66

The Corinthians decided to appeal to Sparta, and took with them the Megarians and an unofficial delegation from Aegina, which complained that their autonomy was being infringed.[1] The Corinthians were heard before the Spartan assembly[2] and Athenian envoys were also allowed to speak.[3] Actually the Corinthians had not a leg to stand on; Athens' alliance with Corcyra was legal, so was her action against Potidaea; the Corinthians were in the wrong in supporting Potidaea. The cases of Megara and Aegina were by no means clear; and anyhow the Athenians offered arbitration according to the treaty.

King Archidamus then spoke.[4] He evidently realized that it was hopeless to urge peace, and he therefore pressed for delay, in order to make further preparations for the vast war effort which would be required. Sthenelaidas the ephor made a brief speech[5] which ended with the words: 'Vote then, Lacedaemonians, worthily of Sparta for war, and do not allow the Athenians to become greater, nor betray our allies, but with the help of the gods let us attack the wrong doers'. He then divided the house. On this occasion he was not content with a shouted decision but held a regular division. The majority for war was very large.[6]

Delphi was then consulted and gave the response that if they fought with all their might they would be victorious.[7] The Spartans then summoned a general council of their allies and put the question of war to them.[8] The Corinthians again made a rousing speech,[9] and a vote was taken of every city great or small. There was a large majority for war.[10]

Thucydides in two passages[11] declares that the Spartans in declaring war in 432 were actuated by fear of the growing power of Athens. In the second passage he gives this analysis of the Spartan attitude during the fifty years between the Persian and Peloponnesian Wars. 'The Athenians had established their

[1] Thuc. I. 66–7.   [2] Thuc. I. 68 ff.   [3] Thuc. I. 72 ff.
[4] Thuc. I. 79 ff.   [5] Thuc. I. 86.   [6] Thuc. I. 87.
[7] Thuc. I. 118.   [8] Thuc. I. 119.   [9] Thuc. I. 120–4.
[10] Thuc. I. 125.   [11] I. 88, 118.

empire more firmly and had themselves risen to great power, but the Lacedaemonians, though they were aware of this, did very little to prevent it, but remained quiescent for most of the time, never being quick to plunge into wars unless they were forced to do so, and being to some extent hampered by their own domestic wars, until the power of Athens was manifestly rising and they began to attack the Spartan alliance. Then they could endure it no longer, but decided that they must make a supreme effort and destroy their power if possible.'

This account is rather tendentious. The Spartans were not so reluctant to go to war as Thucydides represents; they promised the Thasians to invade Attica in 465, and were only prevented by the great earthquake, and they voted for war at the time of the Samian revolt in 440, but were restrained by the opposition of Corinth. Thucydides' account moreover oversimplifies and unduly rationalizes the state of Spartan opinion. It is clear that there was a sharp division of feeling in Sparta, and that from time to time one party or the other gained predominance. There was a party, evidently led by King Archidamus, which was willing to accept Athens as a great power and to remain content with supremacy in the Peloponnese. But there were clearly many Spartans who were filled with resentment and jealousy of Athens for having ousted Sparta from her former position of the leading power of Greece. This hostile spirit showed itself long before there was any reason to fear Athens. It first appears in the popular clamour for war when Athens took over the command of the Persian war in 477. It was manifested again in 465. The Athenians had at this time done absolutely nothing to threaten Spartan interests; for they could not be held responsible for the activities of their exiled citizen Themistocles, and had recently at Sparta's request tried to arrest him at Argos. The dismissal of the contingent which Athens had sent at their own request to Ithome is another example of suspicious hostility which seems to have been entirely unjustified.

This incident provoked Athenian enmity, and in the war which followed Athens gave the Spartans some cause for fearing her power. She allied herself to Sparta's traditional enemy in the Peloponnese, Argos; she welcomed a rebellious Spartan ally, Megara; she exercised her sea power to conquer a Spartan ally, Aegina, and to harry Corinth, Epidaurus and Sicyon, and to win over the Achaeans and Troezen. She moreover built up a land power by gaining Boeotia and Locris.

When by the Thirty Years Peace Athens abandoned all her gains except Aegina, Spartan fears ought rationally to have been allayed. Athens was now a seapower only; on land she was overwhelmingly outnumbered by the forces of the Peloponnesian League, and was moreover extremely vulnerable to attack, with Megara and Boeotia in the Spartan alliance. Argos moreover had made a separate peace. There was none the less a party in Sparta which was dissatisfied with the terms of the Peace, and secured the condemnation of King Pleistoanax for failing to crush Athens completely. It must have been this same party that carried the day for war with Athens in 440, when she was distracted by the revolt of Samos, and promised to invade Attica to encourage Potidaea to revolt.

XV

THE ARCHIDAMIAN WAR

THERE followed a futile series of last moment negotiations;
Pericles refused to make any concessions. The Spartans
scored a propaganda success in demanding that the Athenians
should allow 'the Hellenes to be autonomous'.[1] Pericles replied
that they would do so 'when the Spartans allowed their cities to
be autonomous not in a way convenient to them (the Spartans),
but as each wished'.[2]

The Spartan allied cities were in some ways freer than the
Athenian. Sparta exacted no money tribute from them, and they
could not be committed to a war without the consent of the
majority. They were however no more free to secede than were
members of the Delian League, and Sparta intervened as much in
their constitutions as the Athenians did in those of their allies.
Neither Athens nor Sparta dictated their constitutions to loyal
allies—though they might support one party in cases of civil
strife. Elis and Mantinea were democracies, Chios and Mitylene
oligarchies. But whenever a city rebelled the suzerain power
installed the form of government which it favoured. The war
thus took a strongly ideological tone. Democrats in the Peloponnesian cities plotted with Athens, oligarchic parties in the Athenian
cities and oligarchic exiles from them conspired with Sparta.[v]

Neither side showed much intelligence and initiative in their
operations. The Peloponnesians invaded Attica in 431, 430, 428,
427 and 425, but achieved nothing except the destruction of
crops, trees and houses. They besieged Plataea and eventually
captured it after two years, massacring the surviving garrison of
200 Plataeans and 25 Athenians in cold blood. The Athenians

[1] Thuc. I. 139.   [2] Thuc. I. 144.

70

finally reduced Potidaea in 430–429, but were soon faced by the revolt of Mitylene (428). Alcidas, the Spartan navarch, with only 42 ships, spent all his time evading the Athenian fleet, and Salaethus, the Spartiate commander sent to Mitylene, unwisely distributed arms to the populace, whereupon they surrendered to Athens (427). After a famous debate the Athenians decided not to massacre the entire population, but only the 1,000 members of the oligarchic government.

In 427 King Archidamus died. He had been a patriotic, able and courageous king. He came to the throne, as a result of his grandfather's exile, at a time when Sparta's prestige was badly shaken, and he helped to restore it by his victory over the Arcadians at Dipaea.[1] At the time of the earthquake he had rallied the panic-stricken Spartans and restored order.[2] But while he was a patriotic Spartan he was a firm supporter of the Spartan-Athenian alliance. In 457 and again in 446 he either refused to serve against Athens, or was in view of his known sentiments passed over for the command. In 432 he did his best to dissuade the Spartans from going to war, and in 431 he postponed the invasion to the last moment in the hope that a peaceful settlement might be made, and was bitterly criticized by his army for so doing.[3] He was a personal friend of Pericles, and the latter feared that he might refrain from ravaging his estates for that reason. [4]

Meanwhile the Athenians made singularly ineffective use of their sea power. In 431 Pericles mounted a huge naval expedition to raid the Peloponnese, and in 430 another attempted to seize Epidaurus. Neither expedition achieved anything. From 430 to 426 both sides conducted futile operations in north-western Greece, and from 427 to 425 the Athenian fleet operated in Sicily to no purpose.

In the course of the war, in 426, the Spartans planted a colony at Heraclea in Trachis, five miles from Thermopylae and two-and-a-half miles from the sea. It was intended to be a naval base

---

[1] Polyaenus, I. 41. [2] Plut. *Cimon*, 16; Diod. XI. 63–4.
[3] Thuc. II. 18. [4] Thuc. II. 13.

to threaten Euboea and a fortress to hold the road to Thrace. It was peopled by Spartans, Perioeci and other Peloponnesians.[1] In 421 it was attacked by the neighbouring tribes, Aenianes, Dolopes, Malians and some Thessalians, and was so weakened that the Boeotians were able to expel the Spartan governor and take it over.[2]

At last in 425 the Athenians achieved a major success. The Athenian general, Demosthenes, on board a fleet proceeding to Corcyra and Sicily, put in on the west coast of Messenia, and fortified the headland of Pylos as a base for raiding Spartan territory and stimulating Messenian guerilla warfare. The Spartans threw a Lacedaemonian garrison into the offshore island of Sphacteria, and the Athenian fleet blockaded the island. The Spartan government in alarm sent ambassadors to Athens to propose peace and alliance, but the Athenian democratic leader Cleon demanded the cession of Nisaea, Pegae, Troezen and Achaea, and no secret negotiations.[3] The blockade continued, but the winter was coming on and it would soon become impossible for triremes to keep the seas. Nicias, the Athenian general, challenged by Cleon to capture the Spartans, offered to surrender his command to Cleon. Cleon, taking a few hundred peltasts and archers, landed them on Sphacteria and made things so hot for the Lacedaemonian hoplites that the survivors, 292 men out of 420, of whom 120 were Spartiates, surrendered.[4]

This was a tremendous blow to Spartan prestige. Spartiates did not always, like Leonidas and the 300, fight to the death. It also freed the Athenians from further invasions, as they threatened to massacre the prisoners in that case.[5] Next year Nicias followed up this blow by capturing Cythera, the island off the south-east Laconian coast.[6] In the same year the morale of the Megarians began to crack. They had been since 431 excluded from all the harbours under Athenian control, and had been subjected to an invasion by the whole Athenian army twice a year. In 424 the

[1] Thuc. III. 92, 100.   [2] Thuc. V. 51–2.   [3] Thuc. IV. 15–22.
[4] Thuc. IV. 38.   [5] Thuc. IV. 40–1.   [6] Thuc. IV. 53–4.

democratic factions, driven to desperation, tried to betray the city to the Athenians. The Athenians, however, only managed to secure the port of Nisaea.[1]

There was now a reversal of fortune. The Athenians attempted an invasion of Boeotia and were heavily defeated at Delium.[2] Brasidas, a Spartiate of rare charm and diplomatic ability, was given 700 Helots and 1,000 mercenaries by the Spartan government, to try his luck in Chalcidice.[3] He bluffed his way through Thessaly, whose cities were supposed to be allied to Athens, secured the co-operation of Perdiccas, king of Macedonia, and by an adroit mixture of propaganda and intimidation secured the revolt of several Athenian allies in Chalcidice. He finally won over Amphipolis, a city of great strategic and economic importance, and an Athenian colony.[4]

Brasidas asked for reinforcements, but none were sent. There were influential Spartans who were jealous of his success, and the peace party, which prevailed at this moment, were only anxious to recover the Spartiate prisoners and finish the war.[5] Amphipolis would be a useful bargaining counter, but they did not want Brasidas pursue his advantage.

Next year (423) the peace party prevailed, and, as the Athenians were also weary of the war, an armistice was signed for one year.[6] Brasidas, however, who had captured Torone and Scione, the latter a few days after the signature of the armistice,[7] refused to be bound by it, and Cleon was determined to reduce Chalcidice before negotiating. He tried to recapture Amphipolis, but in battle both he and Brasidas were killed.

With the 'two pestles of war' dead the peace parties on both sides gained strength. Nicias, who had hitherto enjoyed an unbroken run of luck, wanted peace before his fortune changed. Pleistoanax, who had returned from exile and was the more important Spartan king, now that Archidamus had died, wanted to run no risks. He was, moreover, it would seem, a supporter of

[1] Thuc. IV. 66–74. [2] Thuc. IV. 89 ff. [3] Thuc. IV. 80. [4] Thuc. IV. 78–88, 102 ff.
[5] Thuc. IV. 108. [6] Thuc. IV. 117–9. [7] Thuc. IV. 122.

peace with Athens. He had been exiled for failing to press the attack on Athens in 446, allegedly bribed by Pericles.[1] The other king, Archidamus' son Agis, did not carry on his father's policy, proving a bitter enemy of Athens. But he had no influence as yet, being very young and inexperienced. The Spartans were moreover deeply disappointed over their own war effort, having expected to overthrow the power of Athens in a few years, if they ravaged Attica, and were very nervous of a Messenian or even a general Helot revolt, with Pylos and Cythera occupied. Moreover, the Thirty Years Peace with Argos, made in 451, was due to run out.[2]

[1] Plut. *Pericles*, 22.   [2] Thuc. V. 14–17.

XVI

THE INTER-WAR PERIOD

THE Peace of Nicias was accordingly signed in 421. According to its terms there was to be a truce for fifty years. The Spartans were to hand back Amphipolis to Athens. The other rebellious cities of Chalcidice were to be neutral, paying reduced tribute to Athens. The Spartans were also to restore to Athens Panactum, a fort on the Boeotian frontier. The Athenians were to surrender Pylos and Sphacteria, Cythera and various other raiding posts in the Argolid, Locris and Phthiotic Achaea. Finally, there was to be an interchange of prisoners.[1]

The treaty was not a success. In the first place four of Sparta's important allies refused to sign. The Boeotians, flushed with their victory at Delium, were not prepared to surrender Panactum. The Megarians, whose oligarchy had recently been purged of all pacifists,[2] were determined to fight on, and had a real grievance in that the Athenians refused to restore Nisaea to them. This was because when they asked for the restoration of Plataea, the Thebans had declared that the city had surrendered voluntarily; so had Nisaea, the Athenians replied. The Eleans had private reasons for wishing the war to go on. The Corinthians had a perfectly genuine grievance in the Athenian refusal to restore Sollium and Anactorium, two Corinthian colonies in the north-west, but preferred to take their ground on the oath of alliance which they had sworn to the Chalcidians, alleging 'an impediment of gods or heroes'.[3]

In the second place the Spartans had made a number of promises which they could only fulfil by a major military effort. They

---

[1] Thuc. V. 18–19.   [2] Thuc. IV. 74   [3] Thuc. V. 17, 30–1.

could not just hand over Amphipolis and the Chalcidian cities, any more than they could force their allies to sign the treaty.

The Athenians won the toss and the Spartans had to take the first step. They sent three envoys to Chalcidice and ordered Clearidas, Brasidas' successor, to hand over Amphipolis to the Athenians. He stated that he could not do so.[1]

The Spartans now proposed an alliance for 50 years between themselves (alone) and Athens. Either party might, with the consent of the other, add new clauses to the treaty.[2] In return for this scrap of paper the Athenians restored the Spartan prisoners from Sphacteria.[3]

The Corinthians now approached the Argives and, arguing that the Spartan-Athenian alliance was aimed at the enslavement of the Peloponnese, suggested that the Argives should invite any city which so wished to form a defensive alliance with them, and appoint a small committee to negotiate secretly. The Argives, seeing their dream of Peloponnesian hegemony on the way to fulfilment, acted accordingly.[4] They were first joined by the Mantineans. They had conquered a part of Arcadia during the war and were afraid that the Spartans would make them give it back.[5]

The Spartans, hearing of this Corinthian initiative, sent envoys to Corinth to protest. The Corinthians repeated their plea about gods and heroes.[6] The Eleans now allied themselves with Corinth and Argos. Their reason was that they had before the war assisted Lepreum in a war against its Arcadian neighbours and had received as their reward half the territory of Lepreum, for which they made the Lepreates pay a talent a year rent. When the war began the Lepreates had appealed to Sparta, which had given in their favour and garrisoned their city.[7]

The Corinthians and Argives next tried to seduce Tegea, but without success. The Corinthians began to fear that they would

[1] Thuc. V. 21.   [2] Thuc. V. 23–4.   [3] Thuc. V. 24.   [4] Thuc. V. 27–8.
[5] Thuc. V. 29.   [6] Thuc. V. 30.   [7] Thuc. V. 31.

be isolated and tried to reinsure themselves by asking the Boeotians to negotiate a truce with Athens (renewable every ten days) for them, such as the Boeotians themselves enjoyed.[1] In the same year King Pleistoanax freed the Parrhasians, whom the Mantineans had subjected, and demolished a fort which they had built in their territory. The Spartans also garrisoned Lepreum with Brasidas' Helots, whom they freed.[2]

The Spartans now asked the Athenians to surrender Pylos or at least to withdraw the Messenians and Helots from it. The Athenians not unnaturally refused the first demand, having so far gained nothing out of the peace and alliance, but acceded to the second.[3] Next year the new ephors elected were hostile to the treaty, and tried to persuade the Boeotians to form an alliance with the Argives and thus bring Sparta into the alliance. As a preliminary step, however, they begged the Boeotians to surrender Panactum to them, so that they could ask for Pylos in return. The Boeotarchs eagerly took up the scheme, but they had to refer it to the quadruple federal council of Boeotia, which failed to understand its Machiavellian character, but insisted on standing true to Sparta.[4]

The Spartans again tried to get the Boeotians to give up Panactum, but the Boeotians said that they would not do so unless they were accorded a special alliance like Athens. The Spartans, though this was contrary to their treaty, yielded. The Boeotians proceeded to demolish Panactum.[5]

Next year the Argives, hearing of these events, inferred that the Spartans, Athenians and Boeotians, and for some reason Tegea, were ganging up against them. They immediately became extremely alarmed and proposed a truce of 50 years to Sparta; to save their face they insisted on inserting a clause whereby either party might challenge the other to a battle of champions about Cynuria. The Spartans, thinking it a silly joke, consented.[6]

---

[1] Thuc. V. 32.   [2] Thuc. V. 33–4.   [3] Thuc. V. 35.
[4] Thuc. V. 36–8.   [5] Thuc. V. 39.   [6] Thuc. V. 40–1.

Meanwhile the Spartan envoys returned to the Athenians the prisoners taken by the Boeotians and ceded to them the demolished fortress of Panactum. The Athenians were furious, and more so when the Spartan-Boeotian alliance leaked out. Alcibiades, who had a private grievance against the Spartans, because they had not negotiated through him their official *proxenus*, but through Nicias and Laches, sent privately to the Argives, urging them to send envoys to Athens with the Mantineans and Eleans.[1]

The Spartan envoys, Philocharidas, Leon and Endius, stated in the Athenian council that they had come with full powers. Alcibiades represented to them that if they said the same thing in the assembly they might be exposed to embarrassment, and on his suggestion they told the Athenian people that they had not full powers.[2] Exasperated, the Athenians voted for alliance with Argos, Mantinea and Elis.[3]

At the Olympia this year (420) the Spartans were excluded, and a Spartan chariot-owner, Lichas the son of Arcesilaus, whose team won under Boeotian colours, was beaten by the stewards.[4] Next year Alcibiades, being one of the generals, brought a small force of Athenian hoplites and archers to the Peloponnese, and persuaded the people of Patrae to build long walls to the sea.[5] In the same year there was a war between Argos and Epidaurus. The Spartan king Agis led the Spartans in full force to the frontier, but turned back when the omens were unfavourable.[6] There were also fruitless attempts to hold a peace congress.[7] Next winter the Spartans succeeded in getting 300 men into Epidaurus by sea.[8]

Next summer the Spartans made a more serious attempt to rescue Epidaurus. Under the leadership of king Agis they marched in full force (with all the Helots) to Argos, and with them marched the Tegeates and other Arcadian allies. The other Peloponnesian allies, 5,000 Boeotian hoplites and as many light armed, with

[1] Thuc. V. 42-3.　　[2] Thuc. V. 44-6.　　[3] Thuc. V. 47.　　[4] Thuc. V. 49-50.
[5] Thuc. V. 52.　　　[6] Thuc. V. 53-4.　　[7] Thuc. V. 55.　　[8] Thuc. V. 56.

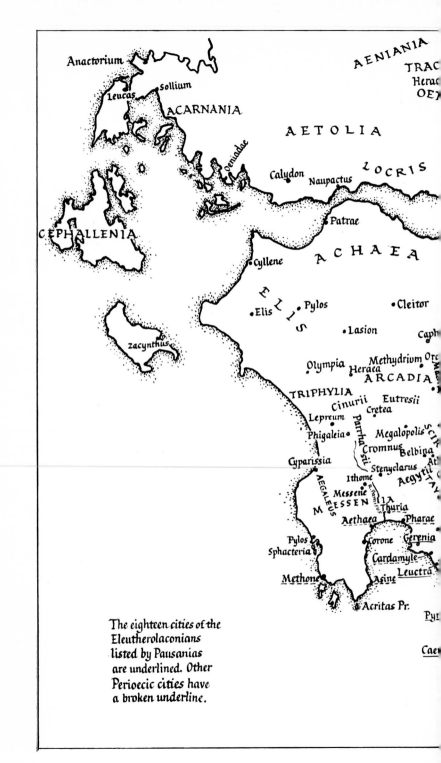

Anactorium

Leucas   Sollium

ACARNANIA

Oeniadae

AETOLIA

AENIANIA

TRAC
Herac
OET

LOCRIS

Calydon   Naupactus

•Patrae

CEPHALLENIA

•Cyllene

ACHAEA

Zacynthus

E L I S

•Elis   •Pylos

•Lasion

•Cleitor

Caph

•Olympia   Methydrium   Orc
Heraea
ARCADIA

TRIPHYLIA

Cinurii   Eutresii
Cretea

Lepreum

Phigaleia •

Megalopolis

Cromnus   Belbina

Stenyclarus

Cyparissia

Ithome

Messene

MESSEN

AEGALEUS

Aethaea

Thuria

Pharae

Gerenia

Corone

Pylos
Sphacteria

Cardamyle

Methone

Asine   Leuctra

•Acritas Pr.

Pyr

Cae

The eighteen cities of the
Eleutherolaconians
listed by Pausanias
are underlined. Other
Perioecic cities have
a broken underline.

Histiaea
Oreus
Scyros

Opus
LOCRIS
EUBOEA

CIS
Orchomenus
Chaeronea
Lake Copais
Chalcis
Eretria
Coronea Halyartus
Aulis
BOEOTIA
Tanagra
Thespiae
Delium
Leuctra
Oenophyta
Plataea Panactum
Eleutherae
Cithaeron
Oenoe
Decelea
Pegae
Marathon
ATTICA

Eleusis
Megara
Athens
Crommyon
Lechaeum Sidus Nisaea
Peiraeus
Corinth Cenchreae
Salamis
Carystus

lius
Nemea
CEOS

Heraeum
Aegina
GOLIS Epidaurus
Argos Cleonae
Nauplia
Troezen
Hermione
Thyrea
Halieis
URIA
Prasiae
Marios
aris
ronthrae
NIA
Helos
Zarax
eum Acriae
MELOS
Asopus Epidaurus
Limera
one
Boiae
Malea Pr.
Pr.
Cythera

500 horse and as many infantry with them, 2,000 Corinthians and the Phliasians in full force, mustered at Phlius.[1]

The Argives with the Mantineans and 3,000 Eleans advanced to Methydrium in Arcadia. Agis broke camp at night and marched to Phlius, and thence by an unexpected route with his Lacedaemonians and Arcadians and Epidaurians into the plain of Argos. The Boeotians, Megarians and Sicyonians were ordered to march towards Argos by the Nemea road, and the Corinthians, Pellenians and Phliasians by another route. The Argives returned to their city to find themselves between three armies, but curiously enough were confident of victory. A different view was taken by Thrasylus, one of their five generals, and Alciphron, *proxenus* of the Spartans. They privately approached Agis with the offer that the Argives would submit their quarrel with Sparta to arbitration and make a truce. Agis accepted this offer without consulting anyone except one officer, and signed a truce for four months. Thrasylus for his pains had his property confiscated.[2] An Athenian force of 1,000 hoplites and 300 cavalry now arrived at Argos under the command of Laches and Nicostratus. The Argives were at first unwilling to admit them in view of their truce with Sparta, but in the end Alcibiades, who was present as ambassador, persuaded them to move against Orchomenus. The Orchomenians joined the alliance, gave hostages to Mantinea and surrendered the Arcadian hostages whom the Spartans had entrusted to them.[3]

On this news the Spartans voted to demolish Agis' house and fine him 10,000 drachmae. They relented, however, but passed a law appointing ten advisers for Agis, without whose consent he might not move an army from the city.[4] Meanwhile the Argives and their allies deliberated what to do next. The Eleans wanted them to march on Lepreum, and when the Mantineans, Argives and Athenians voted against this move, marched off in a huff.[5]

[1] Thuc. V. 57.   [2] Thuc. V. 58–60.   [3] Thuc. V. 61.
[4] Thuc. V. 63.   [5] Thuc. V. 62.

The three remaining allies marched on Tegea. In response Agis occupied Orestheion, with the full levy of Lacedaemonians and Helots. Advancing to Tegea he was joined by his other Arcadian allies. The Corinthians, Boeotians, Phocians and Locrians were ordered to muster at Mantinea. The two armies drew up for battle, the 600 Sciritae on the left wing, next Brasidas' men and the Neodamodeis, about 500 men; in the centre the six Lacedaemonian *morae*, numbering about 6,000 in all, and after them the Heraeans, Maenalians, and on the right wing the Tegeates and a few more Lacedaemonians. On the other side the Mantineans held the right wing, the Argives the centre, with the Cleonaeans and Orneatae, and the Athenians the left wing. The usual speeches were made. The Argives were urged to fight for their ancient supremacy over the Peloponnese, the Mantineans for empire or slavery, the Athenians for the security of their own empire.[1]

Lacedaemonian discipline and training prevailed. They and their allies suffered only about 300 casualties, the Argives and their allies lost 1,100 men. The victory completely restored Spartan prestige.[2] Too late the 3,000 Eleans arrived on the field together with 1,000 additional Athenians. The allies marched to Epidaurus and proceeded to blockade it.[3]

Next winter Lichas, the Spartan *proxenus* of Argos, arrived at the city offering the choice of war or peace. The pro-Spartan oligarchic faction at Argos persuaded the Argive people to accept the terms already voted by the Spartan assembly. These were that the Argives should surrender various groups of Arcadian hostages which they held, evacuate Epidaurus, and make war on Athens if they refused to do the same. On these terms they were admitted to the Peloponnesian alliance on the usual terms.[4]

Shortly afterwards they renounced their alliance with Mantinea, Athens and Elis and made a truce and alliance with Sparta for fifty years. In this document Argos and Sparta shared the hegemony

[1] Thuc. V. 64–9.   [2] Thuc. V. 70–4.   [3] Thuc. V. 75.   [4] Thuc. V. 76–7.

of the Peloponnese: 'and if there shall be need for a common expedition, the Lacedaemonians and the Argives shall take council together judging as justly as possible for their allies. And if there are any disputes between the cities either within the Peloponnese or outside the Peloponnese, whether about boundaries or any other thing, they shall be judged. And if any city of the allies strive with another city, they shall go to whatever city both the cities decide.'[1]

Mantinea now surrendered her conquests, and 1,000 Spartans marched to Sicyon and reduced the numbers of the ruling oligarchy. These Spartans, with 1,000 Argives, next proceeded to install a pro-Spartan oligarchy in Argos.[2] Next summer (417) the Argive people rose and expelled or massacred the oligarchs. The Spartans hesitated and the Argive people was thus enabled, with the aid of Athenian masons, to build long walls joining their city to the sea.[3] Next winter Agis led the Peloponnesian army against Argos and captured the half-finished walls and demolished them.[4] In the following summer (416) Alcibiades sailed with twenty ships to Argos and interned 300 Argives suspected of Spartan sympathies in islands under Athenian control.[5]

In 415 Corinthian and Syracusan envoys arrived at Sparta and with them Alcibiades. The Corinthians and Syracusans asked for help for the latter city, which had been attacked by Athens. Alcibiades, having been indicted for sacrilege by the Athenians, had deserted their cause, and now devoted all his energies to helping their enemies. He made a vigorous speech in the Spartan assembly and persuaded it to send Gylippus, son of Cleandridas, as commander to Syracuse.[6]

Next year (414) the Spartans invaded the Argolid and the Argives invaded Cynuria.[7] In the same summer the Spartans and their allies again invaded the Argolid, and the Argives persuaded an Athenian fleet to make landings at Epidaurus Limera

[1] Thuc. V. 78–9. [2] Thuc. V. 81. [3] Thuc. V. 82. [4] Thuc. V. 83.
[5] Thuc. V. 84. [6] Thuc. VI. 88–93. [7] Thuc. VI. 95.

and Prasiae in Laconian territory and ravage their lands.[1] Under the curious Greek laws of war the Athenians and the Spartans, though they had met in battle, were still at peace and indeed allies.

This greatly cheered the Spartans, for they thought 'that in the previous war the illegality had been rather on their side, because the Thebans had entered Plataea during the truce, and it was stated in the earlier treaty that they were not to resort to arms if the others were willing to submit to arbitration, and they themselves had refused when the Athenians challenged them to do so. And they considered that their misfortunes were accountable for this reason, when they thought about their disaster at Pylos and their other failures'. They accordingly, following Alcibiades' advice, made preparations that winter for the fortification of Decelea in Attica, collecting iron and tools from their allies.[2] In the following year (413) they invaded Attica in full force and built their fort.[3]

At the same time they selected 600 hoplites from the Helots and Neodamodeis and despatched them to Sicily. The Boeotians also sent 300; these sailed from Taenarum in Laconia. The Corinthians also raised 500 hoplites and the Sicyonians 200, and the Corinthians manned 25 triremes to convoy them past Naupactus.[4]

[1] Thuc. VI. 105. [2] Thuc. VII. 18. [3] Thuc. VII. 19. [4] Thuc. VII. 19.

XVII

THE IONIAN WAR

IN the winter of 413–412 the news of the great Athenian disaster in Sicily came through. Athens seemed down and out. The greater part of her fleet was destroyed, she had lost many thousands of hoplites and seamen, and the treasury was empty save for the reserve fund of 1,000 talents. All over the Athenian empire oligarchic malcontents began to stir, preparing revolts and negotiating with Sparta. The Great King's satraps also saw their opportunity.

Both Athens and Sparta were by this time fairly cynical about 'medizing'. Early in the war the Spartans had sent ambassadors to the Great King to ask for money and aid, but they had been intercepted in Thrace and executed.[1] After the death of Artaxerxes the Athenians had sent envoys to the new king, Darius II, and had renewed the Peace of Callias;[2] by this treaty the autonomy of the Greek cities in Asia was guaranteed, and the Persian king promised not to send a fleet into the Aegean. Since then, however, the Athenians had supported a Persian rebel, Amorges son of Pissuthnes,[3] and Darius evidently regarded the treaty as violated, and was pressing his satraps, Tissaphernes in Ionia and Pharnabazus in Phrygia, to collect the tribute from the Greek cities of Asia.[4]

The Spartans began to build 25 ships and ordered the Boeotians to do the same: the Phocians and Locrians were to build 15, the Corinthians another 15, the Arcadians, Pellenians and Sicyonians 10, and the Megarians and the Argolic cities another 10.[5] Meanwhile agents from the Euboean cities approached Agis at Decelea,

[1] Thuc. II. 67. [2] Andocides, III. 29. [3] Andocides, l.c. cf. Thuc. VIII. 5.
[4] Thuc. VIII. 5. [5] Thuc. VIII. 3.

followed by others from Lesbos; to the latter Agis promised support.[1] The Chians, with an envoy from Tissaphernes, approached the authorities at Sparta. At the same time two Greeks arrived representing Pharnabazus. The Spartans favoured the Chian proposal, and so did Alcibiades, for the Chians had a considerable fleet, some 60 ships.[2] The Spartans voted to send 40 ships to support them, but this was easier said than done, for the Athenians had by heroic efforts got together a small fleet, and blockaded the Peloponnesian ships.[3] Meanwhile the Chian government refused to commit itself before the Peloponnesian fleet arrived, as they were afraid that their own seamen would revolt and overthrow the government if it took any overt step against Athens.[4]

Alcibiades broke the *impasse* by persuading the ephors to allow him and the Spartan admiral Chalcideus to go ahead with five ships.[5] In the spring of 412 they slipped through and bluffed the Chians into revolt, and after them the Erythraeans and Clazomenaeans.[6] The Athenians sent a fleet to their loyal ally Samos, but despite their efforts Alcibiades induced Teos to surrender and persuaded Miletus to revolt.[7] A treaty was now signed between Tissaphernes and the king on the one hand and the Spartans and their allies on the other, whereby the king was to recover all the territory that his ancestors had ever held, and the two parties were to make war jointly on Athens.[8]

The Peloponnesians and Chians now secured the revolt of Methymna and Mitylene, but when Astyochus, who had succeeded Chalcideus as admiral, sailed there, he found that the Athenians had recovered Mitylene without a struggle.[9] The Athenians also recovered Clazomenae, and established a blockade of Chios.[10] The Samian democrats secured their island for Athens by killing 200 of their aristocrats and exiling 400 more.[11] The

[1] Thuc. VIII. 5.   [2] Thuc. VIII. 5–6.   [3] Thuc. VIII. 6, 10–11.
[4] Thuc. VIII. 9.   [5] Thuc. VIII. 12.   [6] Thuc. VIII. 14.
[7] Thuc. VIII. 16–17.   [8] Thuc. VIII. 18.   [9] Thuc. VIII. 22–3.
[10] Thuc. VIII. 23–4.   [11] Thuc. VIII. 21.

Athenians later reinforced the city with 1,500 of their own hoplites and 1,000 Argives and 1,000 other allies, together with 48 ships. They attacked Miletus, which was defended by 800 of its citizens and the Peloponnesian forces and Persian mercenaries. Victory went to the Athenians, and they proceeded to blockade the city.[1] Then 55 ships arrived under Therimenes to reinforce the Peloponnesian fleet, including 20 from Syracuse and two from Selinus in Sicily. Under this threat the Athenians withdrew to Samos again.[2]

In the following winter (412–411) Tissaphernes began to blow hot and cold. He supplied a month's pay at the full rate of a drachma a day, but then reduced the rate to half a drachma.[3] Later a Spartan commander arrived with ten Thurian, one Syracusan and one Laconian ship and occupied Cnidus, which Tissaphernes had won over.[4] Therimenes negotiated a second treaty with Tissaphernes and the Great King, which expressly bound the latter to pay the expenses of any force operating in his territory.[5]

In 411 the Spartan government sent out Antisthenes with 15 ships to assist Pharnabazus, and with him 11 Spartiates as advisers to the admiral Astyochus with authority to depose him. After various adventures they effected a junction with Astyochus at Caunus. The advisers strongly criticized the two treaties signed with the king, which acknowledged his rule, as they pointed out, even over Thessaly and Boeotia and Locris. While negotiations were pending, Rhodian aristocrats invited the Spartans to seize their three cities, which they succeeded in doing.[6]

Alcibiades had meanwhile established himself with Tissaphernes, and urged upon him that it would be his best policy not to allow the Spartans to achieve a complete victory, but to wear both sides out. With this object in view he should supply the Spartans sparingly with driblets of pay. This was Tissaphernes' own policy, but Alcibiades, by making himself his

[1] Thuc. VIII. 25.   [2] Thuc. VIII. 26–7.   [3] Thuc. VIII. 29.
[4] Thuc. VIII. 35.   [5] Thuc. VIII. 36–7.   [6] Thuc. VIII. 39–44.

spokesman, made it appear his own.[1] On the strength of his supposed influence with Tissaphernes he opened negotiations with Athenian oligarchs, suggesting that if the democracy which had expelled him could be overthrown, he could bring Tissaphernes over to the Athenian side.[2]

The oligarchs eagerly swallowed the bait, and made preparations for a counter-revolution at Athens. Before the coup could come off, it was clearly revealed to them that Alcibiades could not deliver the goods, but, being now committed, they partly terrorized and partly bluffed the Athenian assembly into voting full powers to a council of 400. Though they had persuaded the Athenians to forego their democratic rights on the ground that Athens would thus receive Persian aid against Sparta, their real object was to make peace with Sparta, if possible keeping the empire, otherwise keeping only the fleet and the walls, in the last resort abandoning even these so long as they kept their power in Athens.[3] They promptly opened negotiations with Agis, who did not take them seriously, but hoping to catch the Athenians at a disadvantage owing to their dissensions, made a surprise attack on the city, but without success.[4] Envoys were also sent to Sparta, but the crews of the state trireme which carried them mutinied when they reached Argos, and handed the envoys over to the Argive government.[5]

Meanwhile the Spartan advisers insisted on a new treaty with the Great King. His sovereignty was acknowledged in Asia only. Tissaphernes was to supply the Spartan fleet until the king's fleet arrived. When it arrived the Spartans could either finance their own fleet, or, if they continued to draw upon Tissaphernes, repay the amount after the war.[6] Soon after a Spartan commander, Dercylidas, was sent north by land with a small force, and succeeded with Pharnabazus' aid in detaching Abydos and Lampsacus from the Athenians; the latter, however, was quickly retaken by the Athenians, who established themselves at Sestos.[7]

[1] Thuc. VIII. 45–6.   [2] Thuc. VIII. 47 ff.   [3] Thuc. VIII. 91.   [4] Thuc. VIII. 70–1.
[5] Thuc. VIII. 71, 86.   [6] Thuc. VIII. 58.   [7] Thuc. VIII. 61–2.

Envoys were also sent by the Four Hundred to the Athenian fleet at Samos, representing that the constitution was a moderate one, in which the power was held by 5,000 citizens, and was designed for the more efficient prosecution of the war.[1] The fleet, however, under the leadership of Thrasybulus and Thrasyllus, rejected their advances, and swore to carry on the war and regard the 400 as their enemies: the Samians, having expelled their leaders, who, originally democratic and pro-Athenian, had been won over by the oligarchs, made common cause with the fleet. The sailors proceeded to elect new generals, and recalled Alcibiades, who had been thrown over by the oligarchs.[2] He was elected one of the generals. On his arrival he did a great service to Athens by persuading the sailors not to attack the 400 but to concentrate on the war with Sparta.[3]

Tissaphernes meanwhile was keeping the Peloponnesians on such short rations that the Spartans determined to detach 40 ships and send them northwards to Pharnabazus, who promised liberal subsidies. Ten succeeded in getting through, and caused Byzantium to revolt.[4] The rest of the Peloponnesian fleet at Miletus, infuriated with Astyochus' weakness and Tissaphernes' failure to pay them, mutinied, led by the Sicilian and Italian contingents, and Astyochus had to take refuge on an altar. The Milesians also mutinied, refusing to accept Tissaphernes' rule.[5] Soon after this Mindarus arrived to succeed Astyochus as admiral.[6] Tissaphernes withdrew to Aspendus to take command of the Persian fleet of 147 Phoenician ships, which had mustered there. Henceforth he kept both sides on tenterhooks, but never actually moved this fleet further west.[7]

At Athens the extremists among the oligarchs sent a second embassy to Sparta, apparently offering to betray the city, and set about building a fort at Eetioneia, where they could receive a Spartan landing party.[8] At this juncture a fleet of 42 Tarentine,

[1] Thuc. VIII. 72.   [2] Thuc. VIII. 73–7.   [3] Thuc. VIII. 81–2, 86.
[4] Thuc. VIII. 80.   [5] Thuc. VIII. 83–4.   [6] Thuc. VIII. 85.
[7] Thuc. VIII. 87.   [8] Thuc. VIII. 90.

Locrian and Sicilian ships arrived at Las in Laconia. Their objective was Euboea, whose inhabitants wished to rebel from Athens, but the more moderate Athenian oligarchs, under the leadership of Theramenes, believed, or professed to believe, that Eetioneia was their objective, and provoked a mutiny among the hoplites who were working on the fort. They demanded that the government be handed over to the 5,000.[1] The 42 enemy ships now appeared off the coast of Salamis under Hegesandridas. The Athenians, who were holding an assembly in the theatre of Dionysus, rushed down pell mell to man the coast, and Hegesandridas sailed on to Eretria.[2] The Athenians hastily manned as many ships as they could and with their flotilla in Euboean waters formed a fleet of 36 ships. Not only were they inferior in numbers but they were a scratch lot of ships, and they were utterly defeated, losing 22 ships. All the Euboean cities revolted except the Athenian colony of Oreus.[3]

The fortunes of Athens were at their lowest ebb. The Spartan fleet could have sailed into Piraeus unopposed. But then, as so often, the Spartans showed themselves most convenient enemies of Athens, as Thycydides says. They missed their opportunity through excessive caution.[4]

The Athenians now set up a government in which the hoplites held control. The extremist oligarchs fled to Sparta, one of them betraying the fortress of Oenoe on his way.[5]

Meanwhile on the other side of the Aegean, Mindarus, the Spartan admiral, tiring of Tissaphernes' tergiversations, sailed north with 63 ships to the Hellespont, where he incorporated 23 Peloponnesian ships already on the spot into his fleet. The Athenians followed him northward with 55 ships and joined up with their flotilla of 18 ships at Sestos. A great battle now took place at Cynossema, in which the Athenians were successful, capturing 21 ships and losing 15. This not very striking victory

[1] Thuc. VIII. 91–2.   [2] Thuc. VIII. 94.   [3] Thuc. VIII. 95.
[4] Thuc. VIII. 96.   [5] Thuc. VIII. 97–8.

put new heart into the Athenians, who had lost confidence since the Sicilian disaster.[1]

The Athenian fleet was now reinforced from Athens, which under the new regime was reconciled with its sailors, but it was defeated. The Spartans were next reinforced from Rhodes, and the Athenians by Alcibiades, and a second battle took place at Abydos, in which the Athenians captured 30 ships.[2] They could not, however, exploit their victory, as they had to disperse to collect funds by blackmailing the cities.[3] When they reassembled next spring (410) Alcibiades insisted on forcing a battle at Cyzicus, and the Athenians were completely victorious, capturing all the Peloponnesian ships.[4] Mindarus the admiral was killed and his secretary sent a despatch to Sparta: 'The ships have gone; Mindarus is dead; the men are hungry; we do not know what to do'.[5]

The Spartan government sent Endius as envoy to Athens to propose peace. He put the facts with brutal directness. The Peloponnesians were peaceably cultivating their land, while the Athenians were excluded from Attica. Sparta had gained allies during the war, while Athens had lost them. The Persian king was financing Sparta, while Athens was miserably poor. Above all, Sparta was unbeaten on land. The terms he offered were generous. Both sides were to hold the cities they now held and to abandon the fortresses that they had on each other's territories; prisoners were to be exchanged man for man. The Athenians were persuaded by Cleophon to reject these terms.[6]

Pharnabazus, however, told the Peloponnesians 'not to be discouraged for the sake of timber, as long as their bodies were safe, since there was plenty of timber in the king's territory'. He gave the sailors a garment apiece and two months' pay, employing them as coastal guards, and he told the captains to build ships at Antandros, giving them money and authorizing them to cut timber on Mount Ida.[7] Cratesippidas was sent out to succeed

[1] Thuc. VIII. 101–6.   [2] Xen. *Hell*. I. i. 1–7.   [3] Xen. *Hell*. I. i. 8.
[4] Xen. *Hell*. I. i. 11–18.   [5] Xen. *Hell*. I. i. 23   [6] Diod. XIII. 52–3.
[7] Xen. *Hell*. I. i. 24–5.

Mindarus as admiral.[1] Alcibiades in the meanwhile recovered Cyzicus and Perinthus and established a toll station at Chrysopolis, levying a 10 per cent. duty on all shipping passing through the Bosporus.[2]

In 409 the Athenian general Thrasyllus returned to Athens, and was voted 1,000 hoplites, 100 cavalry and 50 ships; 5,000 of the sailors were issued with peltasts' equipment. He proceeded to Ephesus, but suffered a defeat when he tried to capture the city.[3]

Next year (408) the Athenians took Selymbria and Byzantium and besieged Chalcedon, and made Pharnabazus agree to send envoys to the Great King.[4] On the way inland, however, the envoys crossed a Spartan embassy, who declared that they had got all they wanted from the King, who was sending down his son Cyrus as commander in chief of western Asia Minor to co-operate with the Spartans.[5]

In 407 Alcibiades was elected general at Athens during his absence[6] and returned to the city, receiving a great ovation. He was sent out to Samos with a fleet of 100 ships, 1,500 hoplites and 150 cavalry.[7] At the same time Cratesippidas was succeeded by Lysander, who was both an able admiral and a dexterous diplomat, and established close and cordial relations with Cyrus, and with the oligarchs in the cities.[8] He refused battle to Alcibiades, who went off to join Thrasybulus, leaving his navigating officer Antiochus in charge of the fleet and instructing him to avoid any action. Antiochus was, however, lured into battle by Lysander and lost 15 ships at Notium (406). The Athenians, angered with Alcibiades for his irresponsible conduct, deposed him, and he sailed off to a castle on the Hellespont which he owned.[9]

In the same year (406) Lysander was succeeded by Callicratidas, a generous-hearted but irascible man. He quarrelled with Lysander and made all Lysander's friends in the cities his enemies. Kept

[1] Xen. Hell. I. i. 32.   [2] Xen. Hell. I. i. 19–22.   [3] Xen. Hell. I. i. 34, ii. 1–11.
[4] Xen. Hell. I. iii. 2–20.   [5] Xen. Hell. I. iv. 1–4.   [6] Xen. Hell. I. iv. 10.
[7] Xen. Hell. I. iv. 21.   [8] Xen. Hell. I. v. 1–7.   [9] Xen. Hell. I. v. 10–17.

waiting by Cyrus for his money, he declared that 'the Greeks were in a miserable condition, flattering barbarians for the sake of money, and that if he got safe home he would do his best to reconcile the Athenians and Lacedaemonians'. He sent home for money, and raised funds from the local oligarchs. He then sailed to Lesbos and captured Methymna; he sold the Athenian garrison as slaves, but set the Methymnaean captives free, declaring that, in so far as in him lay, no Hellene should be enslaved.[1]

He defeated the Athenian admiral Conon with the loss of 30 ships, and blockaded the rest of his fleet. When the Athenians heard of this disaster, they made a supreme effort, conscripting all men of military age and freeing their slaves, and in thirty days manned a fleet of 110 ships. This fleet picked up 40 other ships from Samos and sailed for Lesbos. At the battle of Arginusae it was victorious; the Spartans lost over 70 ships, the Athenians 25. Callicratidas was killed in action.[2]

Again the Spartan government proposed peace to Athens, offering to evacuate Decelea and suggesting that otherwise the two parties should keep what they held. The Athenian politician Cleophon persuaded the people to reject this offer.[3] He may well have been right, for feelings were so exacerbated among the Spartan allies that she could not have imposed peace on them any more than in 421.

The Spartan government now (405) decided to put Lysander in command again, but as the law forbade the same man to serve as admiral twice, they appointed Aracus as navarch and made Lysander himself his secretary.[4] Lysander proceeded to Ephesus, where he set about building more ships. He was then summoned by Cyrus, who told him that his father Darius was seriously ill and had sent for him. He accordingly handed over to Lysander all the surplus money, and assigned to him the revenues of the cities which had been allocated to himself.[5] Lysander first moved to Rhodes and then sailed north to the Hellespont with 200 ships,

[1] Xen. *Hell.* I. vi. 1–16.   [2] Xen. *Hell.* I. vi. 17–35.   [3] Arist. *Resp. Ath.* 34. 1.
[4] Xen. *Hell.* II. i. 7.   [5] Xen. *Hell.* II. i. 10–14.

and capturing Lampsacus, anchored there. The Athenians, with 180 ships, took up their station opposite on the open beach of Aegospotami.[1] For four successive days they launched their ships in the morning and challenged Lysander to battle, but he refused to come out. Each day they returned to Aegospotami in the afternoon, beached their ships, and scattered to make their meal. Alcibiades, who was living close by, warned the Athenian generals of the risk of occupying an open beach and urged them to move to Sestos, but they rudely replied that he was not a general and they were. On the fifth day Lysander swooped with all his fleet on the beached Athenian ships while the men were dispersed cooking and eating, and captured every one except eight which were under the immediate command of Conon, and the state despatch ship, the Paralos.[2] Conon made off to Cyprus, the Paralos carried the news of the disaster to Athens.[3] Lysander, having sent a despatch to Sparta, rounded up the Athenian crews and massacred them. He then sailed in a leisurely fashion towards Athens, reducing the remaining Athenian allies on the way;[4] only Samos resisted stubbornly.[5] Everywhere he installed decarchies, committees of ten local oligarchs, often his friends, with a Spartan governor (harmost) and a garrison.[6] [w] He allowed the Athenian garrisons and settlers to sail back to Athens, in order to swell the numbers in the city and hasten the oncome of famine.[7]

Agis was at Decelea as usual. The other Spartan king, Pausanias, marched into Attica with the Peloponnesian levies. Lysander himself anchored with his 200 ships off Piraeus.[8] The Athenians sent envoys to Agis asking for peace, offering to become allies of Sparta, still holding their walls and the Piraeus. Agis referred them to Sparta, but the envoys were turned back at the Laconian frontier by the ephors, and ordered to bring a better offer—it was suggested that the long walls must be demolished.[9]

[1] Xen. *Hell*. II. i. 15–21. [2] Xen. *Hell*. II. i. 22–8. [3] Xen. *Hell*. II. i. 29.
[4] Xen. *Hell*. II. i. 30–2. [5] Xen. *Hell*. II. ii. 6. [6] Plut. *Lys*. 5, 13.
[7] Xen. *Hell*. II. ii. 1–2. [8] Xen. *Hell*. II. ii. 7–8. [9] Xen. *Hell*. II. ii. 11–13.

The democratic leader Archestratus was arrested for proposing to accept these terms, and a resolution was passed that it should be illegal to propose such a measure.[1]   Theramenes then offered to go and treat with Lysander. He stayed with him three months, until the famine in Athens was acute, and then returned in 404 and announced that envoys must be sent with full powers to Sparta. He was sent with nine others, and the ephors admitted them.[2] A general council of the Peloponnesian league was held, and many of the allies, especially the Corinthians and Boeotians, demanded that Athens should be utterly destroyed. The Spartans, however, declared 'that they would not sell into slavery a Greek city which had done great things for Hellas in its hour of greatest peril'.[3]

[1] Xen. *Hell*. II. ii. 15.   [2] Xen. *Hell*. II. ii. 16–19; Lysias, XII. 68 ff., XIII. 9 ff.
[3] Xen. *Hell*. II. ii. 19–20.

XVIII

AFTER THE FALL OF ATHENS

THE terms offered to Athens were as follows. 'This is the pleasure of the authorities of the Lacedaemonians, that you throw down the Piraeus and the Long Legs, leave all the cities and hold your own land. If you do so, you shall have peace if you desire; and you shall receive back your exiles. About the number of ships do whatever is decided there.'[1] The Athenians perforce accepted these terms; they were allowed to keep twelve ships, and became subject allies of Sparta, bound to follow her leadership by land and sea.[2]

Nothing was said explicitly about the constitution of Athens in the peace terms, except for the clause about the exiles. The Athenians did not receive a decarchy like the other cities, but the 'ancestral constitution' was to be revived.[3] When the Athenian assembly demurred, Lysander sailed back to Athens, and declaring that the peace had been broken, because the Long Walls had not yet been demolished, forced the assembly to 'elect' thirty commissioners with full powers to draw up the constitution.[4] It had apparently been agreed that the oligarchic exiles should nominate ten, Theramenes another ten, while ten should be elected by a free vote of the assembly.[5] Actually all the Thirty seem to have been extreme oligarchs except for Theramenes himself.

The Thirty soon found that they could not control the city without external support, and they obtained a Spartan harmost, Callibius, and a garrison from Lysander.[6] Thus fortified they proceeded to proscriptions not only of leading democrats, but of

---

[1] Plut. *Lys.* 14.   [2] Xen. *Hell.* II. ii. 20.
[3] Arist. *Resp. Ath.* 34. 3, who puts it in the formal terms.
[4] Lysias, XII. 71–6.   [5] Lysias, XII. 76.   [6] Xen. *Hell.* II. iii. 13–14.

T

MACEDONIA

ELIMIA

CHALCIDICE

Amphipolis

THASOS

SAMO

R. Strymon

R. Axios

Spartolus

Apollonia

Olynthus

Acanthus

Potidaea

Mende

Torone

Scione

AEGEAN

LEMNO

Corcyra

EPIRUS

Dodona

THESSALY

Larissa

Pherae

Pagasae

Ambracia

Tempe

ACHAEA
PHTHIOTIS

Anactorium

Sollium

Leucas

ACARNANIA

DOLOPIA

MALIS

Heraclea

DORIS

LOCRIS

Histiaea

Oreus

SCYROS

AETOLIA

Delphi

LOCRIS

PHOCIS

Orchomenus

EUBOEA

Naupactus

BOEOTIA

Chalcis

CEPHALLENIA

Patrae

Coronea

Thebes

Eretria

ACHAEA

Tanagra

ATTICA

Zacynthus

ELIS

Sicyon

Megara

Athens

Carystus

Elis

ARCADIA

Phlius

Corinth

Peiraeus

IONIAN SEA

Orchomenus

ARGOLIS

Argos

Salamis

SARONIC GULF

Andros

Mantinea

Epidaurus

Aegina

CEOS

TRIPHYLIA

Tegea

Troezen

Megalopolis

Hermione

Messene

LACONIA

MESSENE

Sparta

Paros

Gytheum

The

Cydonia

CRE

Cn
Ly
Gor

GREECE AN

C E

BOSPORUS

Selymbria
Perinthus Byzantium Chrysopolis
Chalcedon

PROPONTIS

BITHYNIA

PAPHLA

GONIA

R. Sangarias

...tam...
Lampsacus Cyzicus
Sestos Colonae
Abydos

PHRYGIA

TROAS

MYSIA

R. Macestus

R. Caicus

ssa
Mytilene

Arginus...

LYDIA

R. Hermus

Phocaea

Synnada

Clazomenae Sardis

Erythrae
Teos

Notium
Ephesus

R. Maeander

AMOS

MYCALE

Samos

Alabanda

Miletus

Iasos

Amblada

CARIA

Cibyra

Sagalassus

Cos

Selge

Cnidus

Caunus

Aspendus

Nisyros

PAMPHYLIA

LYCIA

Lalysus Rhodus
Camirus

RHODES

Lindus

Carpathos

non-political rich men, including resident foreigners, and finally excluded from Athens, and as far as they could from Attica, all except 3,000 of the wealthier citizens. Feeling among the Boeotians and Megarians began to change, and they harboured the Athenian exiles and gave them aid.[1]

Soon a group under Thrasybulus, using Boeotia as their base, seized the fortress of Phyle, and occupied Piraeus, which was deserted. The Thirty tried to expel them, but were beaten off and their leader, Critias, killed.[2] The 3,000 deposed the Thirty, who with a few followers established themselves at Eleusis, whose inhabitants they had previously massacred.[3] They asked for Spartan aid, and so did the board of Ten, whom the 3,000 elected to replace them.[4]

Lysander in response to this appeal got himself appointed harmost for Athens, and his brother Libys navarch, and blockaded Piraeus by land and sea. But King Pausanias was jealous of Lysander's power and disagreed with his policy, and persuaded three of the ephors to call up the levy and put him in command. The Corinthians and Boeotians refused to send contingents. They had perhaps undergone a change of heart since they urged the destruction of Athens; but if Athens was to continue, they did not want it to be a puppet state of Sparta and a threat to themselves.[5]

Pausanias inflicted a sharp defeat on the Athenian democrats in the Piraeus, and then invited them and the 3,000 to send delegates to arrange a settlement.[6] It was agreed (403) that the Thirty, with any Athenians who wished to join them, should occupy Eleusis as a separate state, and that the other Athenians should keep the rest of Attica. Both cities were to be allies of Sparta, and there was to be an amnesty except for the leaders.[7] It was a statesman-like settlement, even if it was advantageous to Sparta that Attica should be partitioned. Actually the division only lasted two years,

[1] Xen. *Hell.* II. iv. 1, cf. *Hell. Oxy.* xii. 1.   [2] Xen. *Hell.* II. iv. 2–12, 18–19.
[3] Xen. *Hell.* II. iv. 23–4.   [4] Xen. *Hell.* II. iv. 28.   [5] Xen. *Hell.* II. iv. 28–30.
[6] Xen. *Hell.* II. iv. 31–6.   [7] Xen. *Hell.* II. iv. 38; Arist. *Resp. Ath.* 39.

and in 401 Athens was reunited under a democratic régime, and the amnesty faithfully observed.[1]

There were many influential persons in Sparta who disapproved of Pausanias' mildness. On his return he was arraigned before the *gerusia* and the ephors. The twenty-eight elders were evenly divided and Agis voted against his colleague. But the five ephors all voted for Pausanias and he was acquitted.[2]

The Spartans were now at the height of their power. They were the acknowledged leaders not only of the old Peloponnesian League but of Athens and of the former Athenian allies in the islands of the Aegean and in Thrace. They possessed a great fleet, and they were moreover very rich. Lysander had paid into the Spartan treasury 470 talents which were left over from Cyrus' subsidy[3] and the former Athenian allies paid an annual tribute which amounted, it was said, to 1,000 talents.[4]

The only blot on their reputation was that they had surrendered the Greek cities of Asia to the Persian king, and this fault was soon remedied. On his father's death Cyrus determined to make a bid for the Persian throne, which had passed to his half-brother Artaxerxes. He hired 10,000 Greek mercenaries and asked Sparta for aid. The Spartans instructed their navarch Samius to assist him and he did so.[5] Cyrus was however killed, and the Spartan government took the view that its obligations to Persia were cancelled. They accordingly in 400 appointed Thibron in command, and sent him with 1,000 Neodamodeis and 4,000 allied troops to free the Greek cities in Asia, where he hired the survivors of the Ten Thousand.[6] Next year he was succeeded by Dercylidas, who continued the war for two years,[7] and eventually agreed to a truce with the satraps Tissaphernes and Pharnabazus, on the terms that the king would leave the Greek cities independent if the Spartans would withdraw their troops and harmosts: these

[1] Xen. *Hell.* II. iv. 43; Arist. *Resp. Ath.* 40. 4.   [2] Paus. III. v. 2.
[3] Xen. *Hell.* II. iii. 8.   [4] Diod. XIV. 10.   [5] Xen. *Hell.* III. i. 1.
[6] Xen. *Hell.* III. i. 4–7, cf. ii. 7, 18, iv. 20.   [7] Xen. *Hell.* III. i. 8–ii. 19.

terms were to be referred for ratification to the Great King and to the Spartan government.[1]

Meanwhile in 401 the Spartans at home proceeded to discipline Elis, which had remained independent ever since the battle of Mantinea. They were charged with having allied themselves with the Athenians and Mantineans, of having excluded the Spartans from the Olympia and flogged the aged Spartiate Lichas, and of having refused to allow King Agis to sacrifice at Olympia in thanksgiving for the victory over Athens.[2] The ephors and the Spartan assembly voted that the Eleans should grant independence to their subject cities, and on their refusal the ephors proclaimed a levy.[3] King Agis invaded Elis, but there was an earthquake and he withdrew from superstitious fear. Next year (400) he again led the levy of the Peloponnesian League (except the Corinthians and Boeotians) into the territory of Elis. Lepreum and five other subject cities of Elis revolted and Agis made his postponed sacrifice to Zeus.[4] An oligarchic revolution now broke out in Elis, but the people, discovering that their leader Thrasydaeus had not been killed by the insurgents, rallied and threw them out. Agis left the exiled Eleans with a Spartan harmost and a garrison in a neighbouring town and disbanded his army. Next summer (399), wearied out by the pillaging of the country by the exiles, the Eleans agreed to surrender the subject towns and to become allies to Sparta; but they kept their democracy.[5]

[1] Xen. *Hell*. III. ii. 20.   [2] Xen. *Hell*. III. ii. 21–2.   [3] Xen. *Hell*. III. ii. 23.
[4] Xen. *Hell*. III. ii. 24–6.   [5] Xen. *Hell*. III. ii. 27–31.

XIX

AGESILAUS IN ASIA

SHORTLY afterwards King Agis died.[1] Lysander's position in Sparta had deteriorated in the last few years. He had been denounced by the satrap Pharnabazus to the Spartan authorities, and had thought it politic to go on a pilgrimage to the oracle of Zeus Ammon in Libya, ostensibly to fulfil a vow.[2] The ephors during his absence deposed many of the decarchies which he had set up in the subject cities.[3] It was probably at this time that he toyed with the idea of making the Spartan kingship elective from all Heraclids (of whom he was one), and he endeavoured to get favourable responses from Delphi and Dodona on this question.[4]

After the death of Agis, Lysander thought he saw a way of returning to power. The succession was disputed between Agesilaus, Agis' brother, and his reputed son Leotychidas, whose real father was believed to be Alcibiades. Agesilaus was lame, and a seer produced an oracle telling the Spartans to beware of a lame kingship. Lysander came to Agesilaus' aid, arguing that by a lame kingship was meant a kingship by one who was not a true Heraclid. Agesilaus had received the regular Spartan training, not having been heir apparent, and appeared to be a docile character. When the assembly elected him king Lysander therefore hoped to become the real ruler of Sparta.[5]

In this same year (399) the Spartans took advantage of civil disturbances at their colony of Heraclea in Trachis to re-establish their authority there. They sent Herippidas with an army, and he, having assembled the people, arrested and executed 500 persons.

[1] Xen. Hell. III. iii. 1.   [2] Plut. Lys. 19–20.
[3] Xen. Hell. III. iv. 2.   [4] Plut. Lys. 24–5, Diod. XIV. 13.
[5] Xen. Hell. III. iii. 1–4.

He also beat off an attack by the local tribesmen, the Oetaeans, and expelled them from the city's territory; they were however restored to their homes by the Thebans five years later.[1]

Early in Agesilaus' reign (398) an alarming incident took place. An informer came to the ephors and told them that he had been approached by Cinadon, a man who was not one of the peers, probably an Inferior. Cinadon had taken him to the market-place and asked him to count the Spartiates. He counted the kings, the ephors, the elders and about 40 others, and asked: 'Why do you ask me to count them, Cinadon?' 'Consider them your enemies', was the reply, 'and all the others in the market-place more than 4,000, your allies. And all the Spartiates that are in the villages, one enemy in each place, the master, and many allies.' Asked how many plotters there were the informer said that the leaders were few, but that they were in touch with the Helots, Neodamodeis, Inferiors and Perioeci: 'For whenever there was any talk among them about Spartiates, no one could conceal that they would gladly eat them raw'. Asked about arms he replied that there were plenty of knives, swords, spits, axes and scythes available in the shops.[2]

The ephors did not dare to summon even the 'little assembly', but consulted the individual elders secretly. Cinadon, who was in the service of the ephors, apparently as a member of the krypteia, was sent out with six or seven Spartiates on a pretended mission to arrest some suspect Helots, and was then arrested, and, after revealing his confederates, executed.[3] The incident was alarming, as betraying the small number of Spartiates, but the real danger was not great, since it would appear that the vast majority of Perioeci, Neodamodeis and even of Helots, except the Messenians, were contented and loyal.

This same year a Syracusan who was visiting Phoenicia noted that many warships were being made ready and that some were already manned, and that others were coming in from elsewhere,

---

[1] Diod. XIV. 38.   [2] Xen. *Hell*. III. iii. 4–7.   [3] Xen. *Hell*. III. iii. 8–11.

and heard that a fleet of 300 ships was being prepared. He forthwith reported this to the Spartan authorities. Nothing was known of the destination of the fleet, but it was rightly assumed that it was intended for the Aegean.[1] In fact, Pharnabazus had the previous year persuaded the Great King to appoint the Athenian Conon, who was at the court of Evagoras, king of Salamis in Cyprus, as admiral, and had obtained from the king 500 talents to commission a fleet.[2]

The Spartans were alarmed and summoned a council of their allies to discuss the situation. Lysander, thinking that the Greeks were far superior at sea, and that the exploits of the 10,000 Greek mercenaries who had served under Cyrus demonstrated that easy conquests were possible by land, advised Agesilaus to offer to take the command in Asia, if he were given 2,000 Neodamodeis and 6,000 allied troops; the only Spartans who were to serve were thirty Spartiate advisers. Lysander, who was appointed one of these advisers, hoped to re-establish his influence by getting Agesilaus to re-appoint the decarchies whom the ephors had deposed in the subject cities.[3]

Agesilaus set out in a crusading spirit, and first sailed to Aulis in Euboea in order that he might make a sacrifice there as Agamemnon had done before he sailed to Troy. The Boeotarchs, however, refused him permission and actually broke up the sacrifice when Agesilaus defied them.[4]

When the army arrived at Ephesus, Lysander's old friends flocked to him; things were in a state of flux in the Greek cities, for the decarchies had been deposed but democratic government had not yet been organized, and the oligarchs hoped to recover their power through Lysander's influence. The result was that Lysander's house was thronged, and Agesilaus was ignored, so that Lysander seemed to be king and Agesilaus a private citizen. The other commissioners were indignant and the king was

[1] Xen. *Hell.* III. iv. 1. [2] Diod. XIV. 39.
[3] Xen. *Hell.* III. iv. 2. [4] Xen. *Hell.* III. iv. 3–4.

furious. He systematically refused all requests made with Lysander's backing. Lysander accepted the rebuff quietly and asked to be sent on a mission to the Hellespont; when his year of office as adviser was ended he returned to Sparta.[1]

Having thus asserted himself Agesilaus covered himself with glory for the next two years, waging highly profitable campaigns in western Asia Minor, penetrating as far as Paphlagonia.[2] The Spartans in the meanwhile (396) formed an alliance with Nephereus, the rebel king of Egypt, who promised them in return for their proffered aid tackle for 100 triremes and 500,000 *medimni* of corn. The Spartan admiral Pharax in the same year sailed from Rhodes with 80 ships against Caunus, where Conon the Persian admiral had stationed himself with 40 ships. Pharax attempted to besiege Caunus, but when a large Persian army arrived withdrew again to Rhodes. Conon had, however, been stirring up the Rhodian popular leaders to revolt against the pro-Laconian oligarchy. The rebellion was successful; Diagoras, the oligarchic leader, and his colleagues were killed, a democracy was established, Conon was summoned from Caunus, where he had assembled 90 ships, and the Peloponnesian fleet had to withdraw. The Rhodians and the Persian fleet scored a further triumph by capturing the convoy from Egypt, and securing all the corn which it carried.[3]

Conon exploited this success to gain for himself further authority and more ample funds. He left his fleet in charge of two deputy commanders, both Athenians, and went to Cilicia where he hoped to find the Persian king. Artaxerxes, however, had gone to Babylon, and Conon had to follow him there. Having secured an audience he undertook to break Spartan sea-power if he were allowed as much money as he wanted. The king appointed him a treasurer, with authority to supply him with whatever sums he demanded, and allowed him to choose any Persian whom he wished as his co-commander. Conon chose the vigorous Pharnabazus.[4]

[1] Xen. *Hell.* III. iv. 7–10.   [2] Xen. *Hell.* III. iv. 11–29, IV. i. 1–41.
[3] Diod. XIV. 79; *Hell. Oxy.* x.   [4] Diod. XIV. 81.

XX

THE CORINTHIAN WAR

IT is difficult to hold together a victorious alliance, but the Spartans showed a singular ineptitude in uniting against themselves their two most faithful allies, Thebes and Corinth, their two ancient enemies, Argos and Athens, and most of the former subjects of Athens whom they had freed from her domination, not to speak of Persia. Success had gone to their heads. Instead of trying to conciliate their discontented allies, their only thought was to discipline them by military action, and instead of making their supremacy welcome to the former allies of Athens they imposed tyrannical governments, governors and garrisons on them, and exacted tribute from them. Even with their old allies they were far too ready to interfere with their internal government and impose upon them the rule of pro-Laconian minorities.

The Persian king was naturally anxious to stir up trouble at home against Sparta, and in 396 sent Timocrates of Rhodes to Greece with 50 talents. Timocrates distributed his money among anti-Laconian politicians in Thebes, Corinth and Argos, and Xenophon[1] regards this Persian money as the prime cause of the war which shortly followed. Another contemporary historian,[2] however, gives a more balanced picture. There were in most Greek cities at this time two parties in a fairly even state of balance, and one of these was pro-Spartan and the other anti-Spartan. The difference was sometimes ideological. Democrats were naturally anti-Spartan, since Sparta made it its policy to suppress democracy, and oligarchs were for the same reason pro-Spartan.

But this was not always the case. At Athens oligarchy was not on the political map after the horrors of the Thirty, but the upper

---

[1] *Hell*. IV. v. 1–2.   [2] *Hell. Oxy*. ii.

and middle classes, who had borne the main financial burden of the war and had suffered most materially from it, were profoundly war-weary and therefore wished to keep their treaty obligations to Sparta, whereas the poor, who had benefited from the empire, were willing to take risks to regain it.[1]

At Thebes again, which was a limited democracy, in which the franchise was restricted by a property qualification,[2] the division was not ideological. 'In Thebes, as I explained before, the noblest and most distinguished citizens were in political conflict with one another, and one party was led by Ismenias and Antitheus and Androcleides, and the other by Leontiadas and Astias and Coeratadas. And of the politicians the followers of Leontiadas favoured the Spartan cause, and the followers of Ismenias were accused of being pro-Athenian, because they had been friendly to the democrats when they were exiled, not that they cared about the Athenians. . . . At that time and a little earlier the party of Ismenias and Androcleides was powerful in Thebes itself and in the Boeotian council, but before that the party of Astias and Leontiadas had been prominent, and had had control of the city for some time. For while the Lacedaemonians were at war with the Athenians and were at Decelea with a large body of the allies, this party had more power than the other because the Lacedaemonians were near, and the city was receiving many benefits through them.'[3]

In Thebes, then, the parties were simply the ins and the outs; one enjoyed Spartan favour and the other was therefore anti-Spartan. Nor did Timocrates' Persian money make much difference. 'Yet some people say that his money was the cause of the people in Boeotia and the other cities mentioned above combining, not knowing that they had all been hostile to the Lacedaemonians for a long time and were watching how they could involve their cities in war. For the Argives and individual Boeotians hated the Lacedaemonians because they were the friends of their

[1] *Hell. Oxy.* i. 3.   [2] *Hell. Oxy.* xi. 2.   [3] *Hell. Oxy.* xii. 1–3.

enemies among the citizens, and the people at Athens wanted to rouse the Athenians from peace and quiet and lead them into war and an active policy in order that they might make money out of public funds. And those who wanted to change things at Corinth were some of them hostile to the Lacedaemonians for the same reasons as the Argives and Boeotians.'[1]

The trouble was started by the party of Androcleides and Ismenias at Thebes, who calculated that if the Spartans continued to be supreme they would always be out of power, but that if they could involve Boeotia and Sparta in war, the former would win, because the Persians would supply ample funds and the Argives and the Athenians would come in. They could not overtly persuade the Boeotians to declare war on Sparta; so they persuaded certain Phocians to raid the territory of the Locrians, with whom they had an old boundary dispute. The Locrians retaliated, and the Phocians launched a regular invasion. The Locrians now appealed to Boeotia and Ismenias and his friends persuaded the Boeotians to support them. The Phocians next asked Sparta to forbid the Boeotians to make war on them, and the Spartans did so, demanding that the Boeotians submit to arbitration. The Boeotians refused, and invaded Phocis.[2]

The Spartans welcomed this opportunity of disciplining the Boeotians. They were annoyed with them because they had claimed a tithe of the spoil from Decelea for Apollo, and because they had refused to join Pausanias' invasion of Attica in 403 and had persuaded the Corinthians to do the same, and finally because they had prevented Agesilaus' sacrifice at Aulis. They thought that the moment was opportune, because Agesilaus was triumphant in Asia, and everything was quiet in Greece; they seem to have forgotten the latent hostility of Argos, Corinth and Athens.[3]

They accordingly sent Lysander in advance to muster the Phocians and their other local allies, the Oetaeans, the Malians, and the Aenianes and their colonists at Heraclea, at Haliartus.

[1] *Hell. Oxy.* ii. 2.   [2] *Hell. Oxy.* xiii; Xen. *Hell.* III. v. 3–4.   [3] Xen. *Hell.* III. v. 5.

King Pausanias was to join them with the Spartan army and the other allies on a stated day. Lysander persuaded Orchomenus to secede from the Boeotian League, and Pausanias collected the allies at Tegea. Meanwhile the Thebans sent an embassy to Athens.[1]

In the Athenian assembly many speakers supported the Theban appeal, and although their position was extremely vulnerable, as the Piraeus was unfortified and there were no Long Walls, the people voted for Thrasybulus' motion to fight on the Boeotian side.[2]

Lysander arrived before the appointed day at Haliartus and tried to persuade the city to abandon its Boeotian allegiance. Some Thebans in the city, however, prevented this and attacked. The Thebans moved quickly to protect Haliartus, and a battle ensued in which Lysander's forces were defeated and Lysander himself was killed.[3]

So died one of the most remarkable of Spartiates, a fine general and a superb diplomatist, who could handle Persians, Greek aristocrats and his own countrymen with equal skill. His policy of decarchies, harmosts and garrisons was an unwise perversion of the existing Spartan preference for narrow oligarchies, for the excesses of these puppet governments made Sparta hated and they were too weak to hold down their cities. He seems also to have supported the anti-Theban policy which was to cost Sparta dear. But if his policies were unwise he was a Spartan patriot. Of the bluest blood, a Heraclid, he was personally ambitious, but he always subordinated his own ambition to the cause of Sparta, and obeyed the constituted authorities even when their commands were most distasteful to him. Born in poverty, he handled vast sums of money with scrupulous honesty. He died as poor as he was born, and the wealthy Spartiates betrothed to his daughters found to their disappointment that they had no fortunes, and broke off the matches.[4]

[1] Xen. *Hell*. III. v. 6–7.   [2] Xen. *Hell*. III. v. 16.
[3] Xen. *Hell*. III. v. 17–21.   [4] Plut. *Lys*. 30.

Pausanias arrived on the appointed day and the Athenians on the day after. Pausanias held a council of war, whether to fight or to recover the corpses of Lysander and the other casualties under a truce. Seeing that the forces that Lysander had collected had all dispersed to their homes, that the Corinthian contingent had refused to come, and that the remaining troops were dispirited, the council decided to ask for a truce. The Boeotians refused to grant one unless the Spartans evacuated their territory, and Pausanias agreed.[1]

It was a grave blow to Spartan prestige, and Pausanias was indicted on a capital charge on his return home, for being late at Haliartus, for recovering the corpses by treaty and not by battle, and for sparing the Athenian democrats at Piraeus eight years before. He did not stand his trial, was condemned to death in absence, and withdrew to Tegea, where he afterwards died.[2]

An alliance was now (395) formed between Boeotia, Athens, Corinth and Argos, and was joined by Ambracia, a colony of Corinth, the Acarnanians, old allies of Athens, the Euboean cities, formerly subject allies of Athens, and the Chalcidians, old subject allies of Athens who were friends of Corinth. The Boeotians and Argives proceeded to capture the Spartan colony of Heraclea. The Lacedaemonian inhabitants were killed, the Peloponnesians sent back to their old homes, the city and its territory given to the local Trachinians.[3]

The Spartans in view of this threat sent Epicydidas to recall Agesilaus from Asia. Agesilaus was bitterly disappointed at having to abandon his conquests, but he obeyed his country's call. He left Euxenus as harmost in Asia with 4,000 men to protect the Greek cities, but he and his army are not heard of again, and they were probably soon withdrawn; the cities of Asia thus fell back under Persian rule. The Asiatic cities were invited to send contingents to Greece and many did so.[4]

[1] Xen. *Hell.* III. v. 21–4.   [2] Xen. *Hell.* III. v. 25.
[3] Diod. XIV. 82.   [4] Xen. *Hell.* IV. ii. 1 ff.

Meanwhile at Sparta the ephors proclaimed a levy, and as the other king, Agesipolis, was only a child, the people appointed his guardian Aristodemus as commander. The Lacedaemonians with the Tegeates and Mantineans concentrated at Sicyon, while the Corinthians and their allies occupied Nemea. There ensued a big battle. On the one side there were 6,000 Lacedaemonians, nearly 3,000 Eleans with their neighbours, 1,500 Sicyonians, 3,000 from Epidaurus, Hermione, Troezen and Halieis, besides the Mantineans and Tegeates and Pellenians; in addition 600 Lacedaemonian cavalry, 300 Cretan archers and 400 slingers. On the other side there were 6,000 Athenians, 7,000 Argives, 5,000 Boeotians, 3,000 Corinthians and 3,000 Euboeans; also 800 Boeotian horse, 600 Athenian, 100 Euboean and 50 Locrian, besides Acarnanian, Locrian and Malian light-armed troops. The battle ended in a Spartan victory, but by no means a decisive one.[1]

Agesilaus received the news at Amphipolis, and pressed on through Macedonia and Thessaly despite opposition from the Thessalians, who were allies of Boeotia.[2] When he was on the borders of Boeotia he heard bad news. The Spartan admiral Peisander, with 85 ships, had been completely defeated at Cnidus by Conon and Pharnabazus, the Persian admirals, with 90 Greek and Phoenician ships. Peisander himself had been killed and 50 ships captured. Agesilaus announced to his army that Peisander was dead, but that his fleet had been victorious.[3]

Another great battle ensued at Coronea (395). On one side were the Boeotians, Athenians, Argives, Corinthians, Euboeans, Aenianes and Locrians. Agesilaus had one Lacedaemonian *mora* which had come up from Corinth, half of a *mora* which had been holding Orchomenus, and the Neodamodeis who had been with him in Asia, together with the contingents from the Greek cities of Asia and some from Thrace which he had picked up en route, a body of mercenaries, and Orchomenians and Phocians from the neighbourhood. The battle was more or less a draw;

[1] Xen. *Hell.* IV. ii. 9–23.   [2] Xen. *Hell.* IV. iii. 1–9.   [3] Xen. *Hell.* IV. iii. 10–14.

the Spartan side lost 350 men and their opponents 600.[1] Agesilaus went to Delphi and dedicated a tithe of his spoils to Apollo, and then returned home. Both armies dispersed to their several cities.[2]

Meanwhile Conon and Pharnabazus had been exploiting their victory by winning over the cities of the islands and the Asiatic seaboard from their Spartan allegiance. Conon advised Pharnabazus that if he attempted to make the cities subject to Persia, he would meet with resistance, whereas if he left them independent he would win good will. Pharnabazus wisely followed his advice.[3] Cos, Chios, Nisyros, Teos, Mitylene, Ephesus and Erythrae and others expelled their Spartan harmosts and garrisons. Only Dercylidas, who was in command at Abydos, held the city, and took Sestos. Pharnabazus moved against him by land and Conon by sea, but failed to dislodge him. However, they crossed the Aegean, ravaged the coast of Laconia, and even occupied Cythera, expelling its Lacedaemonian inhabitants and putting in a garrison. They then sailed to Corinth, concerted their plans with the allies, left them money, and sailed back to Asia.[4]

The next year (394) Conon came with his fleet to Athens, and provided money and his crews as labourers to rebuild the Long Walls and the fortifications of the Piraeus; the Thebans also provided 500 masons. Athens was now once again an impregnable fortress.[5]

In the same year the war was resumed in Greece, the Spartans being based on Sicyon and the allies on Corinth. Many of the leading Corinthians began to weaken when they saw their territory being ravaged, while that of their allies was unharmed, and wished to make peace. Their democratic opponents, fearing that they might betray the city to the Spartans, carried out a well organized and ruthless massacre during a religious festival.

[1] Xen. *Hell.* IV. iii. 15–21; Diod. XIV. 84.   [2] Xen. *Hell.* IV. iii. 21–iv. 1.
[3] Diod. XIV. 84; Xen. *Hell.* IV. viii. 1–2.
[4] Diod. XIV. 84; Xen. *Hell.* IV. viii. 3–8.
[5] Diod. XIV. 85; Xen. *Hell.* IV. viii. 9–10.

Many were killed in the first surprise, others fled to altars and statues but were none the less massacred, others again took refuge in the Acrocorinth, which they held against assaults by their fellow-citizens and the Argives who had come to support the democrats. Discouraged by evil omens, however, they abandoned the Acrocorinth and some left the city, while others of them accepted an amnesty proffered by the new government and returned to their homes.[1]

The Corinthian democrats now formed a sympolity with the Argives.[x] Two of the oligarchs within the city escaped through a ravine and made contact with Praxitas, the Spartan polemarch of the *mora* holding Sicyon, offering to let him into the space between the Long Walls joining the city of Corinth to its port of Lechaeum. Praxitas brought up his *mora* together with the Sicyonians and the Corinthian exiles, and established them in a stockade within the walls. Next day there was a confused battle between Praxitas' forces and the Corinthians, a force of Argives who had rushed to defend them, and a body of mercenaries under the Athenian general Iphicrates. In the end the Spartan side prevailed, and Praxitas was able to break down a section of the Long Walls and to capture and garrison two forts in Corinthian territory.[2]

The war continued, both sides using not only their levies but mercenaries. The enterprising Athenian general Iphicrates, using a new type of troops, peltasts, who were more mobile than hoplites, but more effectively armed than the usual light-armed soldiers, so harried Phlius that its people accepted a Spartan garrison; they had hitherto been unwilling to do this because they feared the Spartans would reinstate their pro-Spartan oligarchy whom they had exiled. The Spartans wisely refrained from doing so however. Iphicrates went on to ravage Arcadia, and the Arcadian hoplites dared not face his peltasts. The Spartans retaliated by ravaging Argive territory.[3]

[1] Xen. *Hell*. IV. iv. 1–5.   [2] Xen. *Hell*. IV. iv. 6–13.   [3] Xen. *Hell*. IV. iv. 14–19.

The Spartans, alarmed at the revival of Athenian power, now (392) opened negotiations with Persia. They sent Antalcidas to Tiribazus, the commander-in-chief of the infantry in Asia, and hearing of this move the Athenians sent envoys with Conon and so did the Boeotians, Corinthians and Argives. The terms that Antalcidas proposed were that the Persian king should have the cities of Asia, and that all the other Greek cities on the mainland and on the islands should be autonomous. Tiribazus welcomed this proposal, but the Athenians opposed the plan, fearing that they would thereby be deprived of their cleruchies in Lemnos, Imbros and Scyros, which they had recently recovered, and the Thebans also objected, since it might involve the break up of the Boeotian League, while the Argives feared that Corinth might be separated from them.[1]

This violent change in Spartan policy must have been a grievous blow to Agesilaus, the latter day Agamemnon. He had achieved success and glory in Asia and no doubt hankered for more easy and lucrative campaigns against the barbarians. He had made dispositions when he left Asia which clearly envisaged his early return. Plutarch[2] is surely right in regarding Antalcidas as his enemy, even if his motive was not merely to check Agesilaus' career.

The negotiations broke down, but Tiribazus gave money to the Spartans to commission a fleet, and arrested Conon. He then went up to interview the king. The king, however, sent Struthas down to take charge of the coast, and Struthas, remembering Agesilaus' campaigns, was strongly pro-Athenian. In the following winter (392–391) the Spartans summoned another peace conference. We know of it mainly from a rather tendentious speech by Andocides, who was one of the Athenian delegates. The Spartans offered to insert a clause expressly stating that Lemnos, Imbros and Scyros were Athenian possessions.[3] They insisted that Orchomenus, which had seceded from the Boeotian

---

[1] Xen. *Hell*. IV. viii. 12–15.   [2] *Ages*. 23.   [3] Andoc. III. 14.

League in 395 and had ever since been garrisoned by Sparta, should be autonomous,[1] but apparently allowed Thebes to keep the rest of the Boeotian League. This development of Antalcidas policy must have been even more distasteful to Agesilaus than the original plan, which at least had the merit of humbling Thebes. They also seem to have insisted on the separation of Corinth from Argos. At any rate these cities refused to accept the terms.[2] The Boeotians were content, but the Athenians objecting to the surrender of the Asiatic Greeks to Persia, refused;[3] so that negotiations again broke down. Disappointed in their attempts to placate Persia, the Spartans sent Thibron to Ephesus, but he was killed and his troops routed.[4]

In 390 the Spartans, urged on by exiled Rhodian oligarchs, sent their navarch, Ecdicus, with eight ships, and a general, Diphridas, with orders to rally Thibron's army and the cities which had supported him and to hire mercenaries to fight Struthas. Ecdicus occupied Cnidus, but was unable to effect more until the Spartans sent Teleutias with 12 ships with which he had been operating in the gulf of Corinth to support him. Teleutias picked up seven ships from Samos, which was still loyal to Sparta, and having thus assembled 27 ships, defeated an Athenian admiral with ten ships and established the Rhodian exiles in a fort on the island.[5]

In the same year (390) Agesilaus invaded Corinthian territory. The Argives, representing the Corinthian state as being now Corinthians as well, were beginning the celebration of the Isthmian games, but Agesilaus chased them into Corinth, and stood by while the Corinthian exiles held the games: when he had left they were celebrated a second time by the Corinthians and Argives. Agesilaus then attacked Peiraeum, a strong point where the Corinthians from the countryside took refuge and kept their cattle. The Corinthians abandoned Peiraeum and fled

---

[1] Andoc. III. 13, 20.   [2] Andoc. III. 24 ff., esp. 26, 32.
[3] Philochorus, *FGH* 328, F149.   [4] Xen. *Hell.* IV. viii. 16–19.
[5] Xen. *Hell.* IV. viii. 20–4, cf. Diod. XIV. 97.

to Heraeum, but when Agesilaus attacked them they surrendered at discretion. Agesilaus ordered that those guilty of the massacre of the oligarchs should be surrendered to the Corinthian exiles, and everyone and everything else sold. He also captured another fort, Oenoe, with all its contents.[1]

Whether because of these events, or because they had previously grown weary of the war, Boeotian envoys now arrived to treat for peace. But as Agesilaus was receiving the envoys, a messenger rode up bringing news of a Spartan disaster. It was the custom that all Spartiates of Amyclae should return each year to their native town for the feast of the Hyacinthia. Those in the army near Corinth had been escorted towards Sicyon by a *mora* of infantry and a *mora* of cavalry. When the party were not far from Sicyon the Amyclaeans had been sent forward to the city with the cavalry and the infantry had turned back. Iphicrates, who was in Corinth with his peltasts, with another Athenian general, Callias, with a force of hoplites, decided to attack the *mora* on its return journey. They harried it so effectively that it lost 250 men out of 600.[2]

After this there was no more talk of peace. Agesilaus withdrew to Sparta, passing through the cities after dark to avoid the hostile stares of the populace; the Mantineans were particularly offensive, gloating over the Spartan reverse. Iphicrates was able to recapture the various Corinthian fortresses held by the enemy, Sidus, Crommyon, Oenoe. The Spartans only succeeded in holding the Corinthian port of Lechaeum.[3]

In 389 the Athenians sent out Thrasybulus with 40 ships. He did not attempt to intervene at Rhodes, but sailed to the Hellespont. He promoted a democratic revolution at Byzantium and also won over Chalcedon, and established a toll station to collect money from all ships sailing through the Bosporus. He next moved on Lesbos, where all cities except Mitylene were pro-Spartan, and defeated and killed the Spartan harmost of Methymna,

[1] Xen. *Hell*. IV. v. 1–5.   [2] Xen. *Hell*. IV. v. 6–18.   [3] Xen. *Hell*. IV. v. 18–19.

and won over two other cities, Eresus and Antissa. He then moved south, but was killed trying to collect money from Aspendus.[1]

In the same year (389) Sparta was called upon to fulfil her federal obligations in another quarter. The league of Achaean cities had admitted to membership the Aetolian city of Calydon across the straits, and the Acarnanians attacked the city, assisted by their Athenian and Boeotian allies. The Achaeans protested that they had regularly sent their contingents for Sparta's wars and that Sparta should now help them in their turn. The ephors and the assembly declared war and sent Agesilaus with two *morae* and a contingent of allies, including the Achaeans themselves in full force. Agesilaus demanded that the Acarnanians should abandon the Boeotian-Athenian alliance, and join the Peloponnesian league. When they refused he invaded the country, ravaging it thoroughly and capturing most of the flocks and herds, but failing to take any cities. In the autumn he withdrew, despite the protests of the Achaeans, but promised to return next spring. He kept his word, and, faced by the destruction of another year's crops, the Acarnanians accepted the Spartan terms.[2]

The Spartans next (388) decided to send an expedition to undo Thrasybulus' work in the Hellespontine area. Though they were perfectly satisfied with Dercylidas' conduct the ephors sent out Anaxibius to replace him because he was their friend, equipping him with three triremes and enough money to maintain 1,000 mercenaries. Basing himself on Abydos he raided Pharnabazus' cities in Aeolis, and seized ships passing through the straits. The Athenians countered by sending out Iphicrates with eight triremes and 1,200 of his peltasts. Iphicrates succeeded in ambushing Anaxibius, and killing him and twelve other Spartan harmosts with him, besides 200 of his troops together with 50 Abydenes.[3]

The Spartans also tried to put pressure more directly on Athens sending Eteonicus to Aegina, whence he carried out piratical

[1] Xen. *Hell.* IV. viii. 25–30; Diod. XIV. 94.
[2] Xen. *Hell.* IV. vi–vii. 1.   [3] Xen. *Hell.* IV. viii. 31–9.

raids on Attica. The Athenians counterattacked, besieging Aegina until the Spartan Teleutias arrived with a fleet and raised the siege. The Spartan admiral Hierax then took over, stationing 12 ships at Aegina under his secretary Gorgopas. The Athenians were forced to withdraw from a fort they had built on the island and were subjected to severe piratical raids.[1]

The Spartans were by this time rather tired of maintaining a *mora* at Orchomenos and another at Lechaeum. They were also running into serious difficulties about money, and were unable to pay their crews except from booty and blackmail. They therefore determined to make a final effort to enlist the aid of Persia and to put pressure on Athens to accept a peace on their terms. With this end in view they appointed Antalcidas, who had previously shown his skill in dealing with the Persians, as navarch. He crossed to Ephesus under the escort of Gorgopas' Aeginetan squadron of 12 ships and then sent him back to Aegina. The rest of his ships, 25 in number he sent under his secretary Nicolochus to Abydos, but the Athenian admiral in the northern Aegean, with 32 ships, was able to blockade him there. Antalcidas himself meanwhile went up to see Tiribazus, and arranged a complete accord with him: the Greek king would become Sparta's ally if the Athenians did not agree to the peace. Returning to the coast Antalcidas marched to relieve Abydos. Here he heard the welcome news that twenty ships had arrived from Syracuse and Italy.[2]

The Spartans had maintained friendly relations with Syracuse ever since they had assisted the city to resist the Athenian expedition. After the destruction of the Athenian expedition they had received substantial aid from Syracuse, under the leadership of its republican leader Hermocrates. When Hermocrates fell and was exiled by the Syracusan democracy, and then the tyrant Dionysius established himself, the Spartans continued to keep on friendly terms with the latter, and sent him reinforcements

[1] Xen. *Hell.* V. i. 1–5.   [2] Xen. *Hell.* V. i. 6–7, 25–6.

against the Carthaginians. They allowed no ideological scruples against tyrants to affect their policy, and one Spartan commander in Syracuse, Pharacides, when appealed to by the Syracusan democrats to assist them in overthrowing Dionysius, replied that he had been sent to aid Dionysius and the Syracusans against the Carthaginians, and not to overthrow Dionysius' rule.[1]

The Spartans now reaped their reward in the shape of the 20 ships. Tiribazus and his friend Ariobarzanes supplied more, and Antalcidas thus built up a fleet of 80 ships with which he blocked the Straits and prevented any corn ships from sailing to Athens. Meanwhile the Spartans had sent Teleutias to take over Gorgopas' squadron at Aegina. He had no money to pay his crews, but he was an excellent officer and restored the morale of the fleet, promising them to reward them with booty if they would fight well. He achieved a spectacular success by a daring raid on the Piraeus, capturing vast quantities of shipping.[2]

In the same year (387) the Spartans put pressure on the remaining power which opposed the peace, Argos, with which Corinth was now amalgamated. They voted an expedition against the city and put king Agesipolis in command. The Argives had been in the habit of stopping invasions by manipulating the calendar and declaring a month of sacred truce, binding on all Dorians, whenever an army appeared at their frontiers. Agesipolis took the precaution of consulting Olympia and Delphi on this question and received the reply that he might ignore sacred months unjustly declared. He accordingly ignored the protests of the Argive envoys and marched into Argive territory. Next night there was an earthquake, but Agesipolis remarked that since he had already crossed the frontier this was a favourable sign. He did not achieve much, but by leading his army up to the walls of Argos demonstrated his power.[3]

The Athenians, their corn supply intercepted and their country constantly subject to raids, were now ready to sign. So were the

[1] Diod. XIV. 70.   [2] Xen. *Hell.* V. i. 13–24.   [3] Xen. *Hell.* IV. vii. 2–7.

Argives, with a prospect of renewed invasion. The Boeotians had long tired of the war. There was therefore no opposition when Tiribazos summoned a congress to hear 'the peace sent down by the King'. It ran: 'Artaxerxes the king thinks it just that the cities in Asia should be his, and of the islands Clazomenae and Cyprus, and that the other Greek cities great and small should be autonomous except Lemnos and Imbros and Scyros: and these shall belong to the Athenians as in old times. And whichever side does not accept this peace, I will make war upon them, with those that desire the same, by land and by sea and with ships and with money.'[1]

Agesilaus seems by this time to have realized that the idea of freeing the Greeks of Asia was impracticable, and to have accepted the King's Peace as sound policy: at any rate he acted vigorously to enforce it against his and Sparta's enemies. When some said that the Spartans were Medizing, he is said to have replied that it was rather the Medes who were Laconizing.[2]

[1] Xen. *Hell.* V. i. 31.   [2] Plut. *Ages.* 23.

XXI

THE KING'S PEACE

B Y able diplomacy and by vigorous military and naval action
against Argos and Athens, the Spartans had at last achieved a
settlement highly satisfactory to their interests. The abandonment
of the Asiatic Greeks to Persia was, it is true, rather discreditable,
and Athenian orators from this time forth, led by Isocrates, con-
trasted the glorious peace of Callias, whereby Athens had not only
forced the Great King to respect the autonomy of the cities of
Asia, but had forbidden him to sail the waters of the Aegean,
with the inglorious peace of Antalcidas, whereby Sparta had
betrayed the Greek cities and allowed the Great King to dictate to
Hellas. But the betrayal of the cities of Asia does not seem to
have aroused much general indignation, and the other clause,
guaranteeing the autonomy of all the other cities, evidently
caused widespread approval. Not only did the abstract notion
of autonomy have a strong appeal to all Greeks; to very many
Greek cities, which were either subject to others or in danger of
becoming so, the guarantee really meant something. It was only
the imperialist powers, notably Athens and Thebes, who disliked
the idea. The popularity of the slogan is amply proved by the
numerous subsequent settlements which were attempted on the
same basis.

The Spartans interpreted autonomy in a sense convenient to
themselves. The members of their league were declared in their
treaties to be autonomous; the league therefore was legal and the
allies continued to be *de facto* subject to Sparta. All other leagues
or unions of cities, except those which, like the Achaeans and the
Phocians, accepted Spartan supremacy, were deemed to be in-
fringements of the autonomy of their subordinate members. The

117

Spartans adopted the role of judges and executive officers of the Peace, and no one dared to withstand them. The Thebans, it is true, claimed to sign on behalf of the Boeotians, but when Agesilaus promptly started to muster an army, gave in.[1] The Spartans took the opportunity of refounding Plataea, which they had destroyed forty years before, and the Plataeans, who were residents of Athens with partial citizen rights, returned to their old city.[2] This step was clearly dictated not by any zeal for the autonomy of Plataea, but to weaken Thebes and embroil her relations with Athens. The Argives and Corinthians were also under threat of invasion forced to dissolve their union. The oligarchic exiles returned to Corinth and the democratic leaders fled.[3]

The Spartans now (386) proceeded to discipline their less loyal allies. They demanded that the Mantineans should demolish their walls, declaring that they did not trust them, because they had sent aid to Argos during the past war, had sometimes refused their contingent or sent poor contingents, and rejoiced in Sparta's defeats and been jealous of her victories: moreover the thirty years' truce signed after the battle of Mantinea had run out. The Mantineans refused to obey, and the assembly declared war. Agesilaus refused the command on the ground that the Mantineans had been helpful to his father Archidamus in the Messenian revolt. Agesipolis accepted it, although his father Pausanias had been very friendly with the Mantinean democratic leaders. He first ravaged the land, then built an embankment round the town and blockaded it. But finding that the enemy had large stock of corn, he diverted the river and thus breached the wall, which was of mud brick. The Spartans now dictated severer terms, that the Mantineans should abandon their city and divide themselves into their four original villages. The pro-Argive democratic leaders were allowed to leave under a safe conduct, and an aristocratic form of government was established in the several villages.[4]

[1] Xen. *Hell.* V. i. 32–3.   [2] Paus. IX. i. 4.
[3] Xen. *Hell.* V. i. 34.   [4] Xen. *Hell.* V. ii. 1–7.

The exiles from Phlius, seeing which way the wind was blowing, approached the ephors, who requested the government of Phlius to receive them back. The Phliasians perforce agreed to do so, and to restore to them their real property, and to resolve any disputes arising in the courts.[1]

In 383 envoys from Acanthus and Apollonia came to Sparta, complaining that the powerful city of Olynthus had formed a close federal union with most of its lesser neighbours, including those belonging to Amyntas, king of Macedon, and had demanded submission from themselves. The envoys represented the danger of allowing so great a power to consolidate itself, and declared Athens and Boeotia were already in diplomatic contact with Olynthus. Amyntas, who had surrendered a part of his territory to Olynthus in return for aid against the Illyrians, and having defeated them wanted to recover it, also sent envoys, proposing an alliance. The envoys of the two cities were brought before an assembly of the Peloponnesian league, which obediently to the wishes of the Spartans voted for war and decreed a levy of 10,000 men from the allies. It was, however, proposed that the cities might commute their contingents, paying three Aeginetan obols a day for each hoplite, and two drachmas for each cavalryman. If any city failed to send its full contingent, the Spartans should be authorized to fine it one *stater* (two drachmas) per man per day.[2]

This proposal reflects the growing reluctance of citizen armies to fight in prolonged and distant campaigns. Already during the Corinthian war both sides had come to rely more and more on mercenaries, and this tendency progressively increased. It is not clear whether the present proposal was put in force, but the effect would have been to increase the power of Sparta, which would have commanded ample funds to hire mercenaries and have been less dependent on her allies' goodwill.

The Acanthian envoys demanded more immediate action while the federal army was being mustered, and the Spartans

---

[1] Xen. *Hell.* V. ii. 8–10.   [2] Xen. *Hell.* V. ii. 11–12, Diod. XV. 19.

agreed to send out Eudamidas at once with about 2,000 Neodamo-deis and Perioeci, including the Sciritae. He set out with part of this force, asking the ephors to send on his brother Phoebidas with the rest, and marching to Thrace garrisoned the cities hostile to Olynthus, including Potidaea.[1]

Phoebidas, following him, camped outside Thebes on his way. Here he was approached by Leontiadas, the leader of the pro-Spartan faction in Thebes, who offered to betray the acropolis of the city, the Cadmeia, to him. Phoebidas agreed and Leon-tiadas, having installed him in the Cadmeia, went to the council, and with the aid of military officers in the plot, arrested his rival Ismenias. Ismenias' partisans, about 300 in number, fled from the city to Athens. Leontiadas promptly went to Sparta, placated the ephors, who had at first disapproved of Phoebidas' unautho-rized action, and persuaded the assembly to ratify it.[2] Agesilaus openly lent his support to Phoebidas, declaring that the action itself must be scrutinized, to see what profit it brought; for it was a good thing to initiate what was in the interests of Sparta, even if one had received no orders. The opposition, who included old fashioned men who thought that it was wrong to break oaths, and no doubt sympathized with Thebes, not unnaturally put around the story that Agesilaus had given Phoebidas secret orders.[3] Ismenias was brought before a court of three Spartans and one from each of the allied cities, and condemned to death for accepting Persian money and being a warmonger.[4]

The Spartans now pressed on the campaign against Olynthus, appointing Teleutias as commander and instructing the allies to send their contingents: the Thebans were particularly zealous under their new government. Teleutias wrote to Amyntas of Macedon, asking him to hire mercenaries and buy over the neighbouring kings, and also to Derdas, king of Elimia. Having arrived with all his forces he marched on Olynthus, together with Amyntas' and Derdas' contingents. He won a victory over the

[1] Xen. *Hell.* V. ii. 23–4.   [2] Xen. *Hell.* V. ii, 25–34.
[3] Plut. *Ages.* 23–4.   [4] Xen. *Hell.* V. ii. 35–6.

Olynthians, but had to retire on the approach of winter, while the Olynthians continued to raid the pro-Spartan cities.[1]

Next spring the Olynthians raided Apollonia and Teleutias ravaged Olynthian territory. A battle ensued in which Teleutias was killed and his forces dispersed to Spartolus, Acanthus, Apollonia and Potidaea. The Spartans now put king Agesipolis in command with 30 Spartiate advisers, and sent him to the scene of action with volunteers from the Perioeci and the allies, including some Thessalian horse. Agesipolis marched to Olynthus, again ravaged its territory and that of its allied cities, and stormed Torone. He then caught a fever and died. Polybiades was sent out to replace him, and compelled the Olynthians, who were now starving, to send envoys to Sparta. They accepted the terms offered, to join the Peloponnesian league and accept the Spartan supremacy. The other cities of the district were also enrolled.[2]

In the meanwhile Agesilaus had been yet further humiliating the city of Phlius. The returned exiles came to Sparta complaining that their property claims had not been fairly adjudicated. The Phliasians fined them for going to Sparta without public authorization, and they complained again to the ephors, who declared war on Phlius. The moving spirit behind this severe measure was Agesilaus, who was a personal friend of some of the exiles. He marched promptly, and on receiving offers of peace, demanded that the acropolis be surrendered. Some of the Spartans objected to his antagonizing a city which supplied a contingent of 5,000 for the sake of a few exiles, but Agesilaus overbore them, declaring that the exiles numbered 1,000. Eventually, after a spirited resistance, the Phliasians were starved out, and agreed to submit to whatever terms the Spartan authorities imposed, but refused to treat with their spiteful enemy Agesilaus. Agesilaus however got himself appointed with full powers. He ruled that 50 of the exiles and 50 of those in the city should form a court to decide

[1] Xen. *Hell.* V. ii. 37–43.   [2] Xen. *Hell.* V. iii. 1–9, 18–20, 26.

121

who of those in the city should live and who should die, and to devise the future constitution; until these matters were settled there should be a garrison.[1]

After the King's Peace, as after the fall of Athens, the Spartans were supreme in Greece, and once again power went to their heads. They had, it is true, increased their league by the adhesion of the Thraceward cities, and they had installed subservient governments in Corinth, Mantinea, Thebes and Phlius, but in doing so they had alienated public opinion by their highhanded aggressiveness and their utter lack of scruple. The situation was unstable and it only needed a slight shock to bring down the whole edifice.

In 379 Phillidas, the secretary of the Theban polemarchs, on a visit to Athens met Melon, one of the exiled Thebans. They arranged that six of the exiles should be smuggled into Thebes, and introduced, disguised as women, into a banquet held by the polemarchs. The supposed women refused to come in unless all other men than the polemarchs went out, and thus succeeded in assassinating them all. Phillidas then took three exiles to Leontidas' home; they were admitted and killed him also. This done Phillidas had the prison opened and released and armed the political prisoners. At dawn the party paraded in the market place, and called on the citizens to rise, and they did so enthusiastically. A message was also sent to two Athenian generals who had marched to support the revolution.[2]

The Spartan harmost sent to Plataea and Thespiae, both cities hostile to Thebes, for aid, but only the Plataeans responded, and the Thebans beat them off. Despairing of the situation the harmost agreed to withdraw with his garrison under a safe conduct.[3]

The Spartan authorities executed the harmost on his return and declared war on Thebes. The ephors wisely decided not to put Agesilaus, whose strongly anti-Thebes policy was too obvious, in command of the expedition, but entrusted it to Cleombrotus.

[1] Xen. *Hell.* V. iii. 10–17, 21–5.   [2] Xen. *Hell.* V. iv. 2–9.
[3] Xen. *Hell.* V. iv. 10–12.

The choice was rather embarrassing, for Cleombrotus was probably a strong sympathizer with Thebes. It is difficult to believe that, however incapable he was, his operations against Thebes could have been so inept, unless he wished to spare the city and its territory. He was certainly suspected of undue favour to Thebes by his enemies.[1] The Athenian general Chabrias was blocking the Eleutherae road but Cleombrotus advanced through Plataea to Thespiae, and moved on Thebes. But as the Thebans remained within the walls, he retired after sixteen days and, leaving Sphodrias with one-third of the allied contingents at Thespiae, returned home.[2]

Despite Cleombrotus' unimpressive performance the Athenians took alarm, and condemned the two generals who had supported the *coup* to death. Prudent counsels might have prevailed but for the folly of Sphodrias, the Spartan commander at Thespiae, and King Agesilaus. Sphodrias, hoping no doubt to win credit by a bold unauthorized stroke like that of Phoebidas, attempted to seize the Peiraeus. It was a grossly incompetent action, for when dawn came Sphodrias and his men were only in the Thriasian plain, and as soon as the Athenians were alerted had to withdraw ingloriously.[3]

There happened to be some Spartan ambassadors in Athens at the time, and the Athenians arrested them. They, however, convinced the Athenians that they were not privy to Sphodrias' action, and declared that he would certainly be punished by the Spartan authorities. Cleombrotus' party were anxious to save him, since he was one of themselves; it was even believed by some that Cleombrotus had given him secret orders.[4] Agesilaus was initially very severe against him as a political opponent. Sphodrias did not dare to return to Sparta, but he was none the less acquitted. He had a son who was a lover of Archidamus, Agesilaus' son, and Agesilaus yielded to his son's importunities.[5]

[1] Xen. *Hell*. VI. iv. 5. [2] Xen. *Hell*. V. iv. 13–8. [3] Xen. *Hell*. V. iv. 19–21.
[4] Diod. XV. 29. [5] Xen. *Hell* V. iv. 22–33.

The Athenians were naturally furious and allied themselves with Thebes. Next year the Spartans put Agesilaus in command instead of the feeble Cleombrotus. He saw that it was essential to seize the passes of Cithaeron in advance, while his army was mustering, and, observing that the two Arcadian cities of Cleitor and Orchomenus were at war, and that the former was using a body of mercenaries, he declared that the war must be suspended, according to the rules of the Peloponnesian League, while a federal war was in progress, and ordered the commander of the mercenaries to occupy Cithaeron. He then followed with the main army, and ravaged Theban territory with some success; the Thebans had built a stockade round the central plain, but Agesilaus managed to slip in and destroy the crops within it. This done he returned home, leaving two *morae* to garrison Orchomenus and Phoebidas as harmost at Thespiae to continue harrying the Thebans. Phoebidas was, however, killed in an engagement and his forces defeated, and Pelopidas, with the Theban *corps d'elite*, the Sacred Band of 300 hoplites, caught by the two *morae* at Tegyra near Orchomenus, fought his way through them. This success, which demonstrated that Thebans were as good as Spartans, greatly heartened the Thebans. They pressed their attacks on the other Boeotian cities under Spartan control, and the democrats in these cities deserted to Thebes. The pro-Spartan groups who controlled them found difficulty in maintaining themselves and required Spartan support. Phoebidas was replaced by another harmost who was sent by sea with a Lacedaemonian *mora* and occupied Thespiae.[1]

In the same year (377) the Athenians took advantage of Spartan unpopularity to launch a new league. The preamble of its charter[2] is a magnificent denunciation of Spartan policy and methods. 'In order that the Lacedaemonians may allow the Hellenes to be free and autonomous and live in peace holding all their own territories in security, and that the common peace which the Hellenes and

[1] Xen. *Hell.* V. iv. 34–6.   [2] Tod. *Greek Hist. Inscr.* II. 123.

the King swore according to the treaty may be valid and may continue', the Athenians invited 'any of the Hellenes or the barbarians living on the mainland or on the islands who are not subjects of the King' to join the Athenian alliance, 'free and autonomous, maintaining whatever constitution they wish, receiving neither a garrison nor a governor nor paying tribute'. The response was enthusiastic. The league was joined by Thebes and by a large number of maritime states including Byzantium, Mitylene, Chios, Rhodes and all the cities of Euboea except Hestiaea, which had bitter memories of its past expropriation by Athens.[1]

In the same year the Spartans reorganized their league. It would appear that from the end of the Peloponnesian war they had abandoned the practice of demanding from their allies two-thirds of their total levies, and had asked for contingents of varying size to make up whatever total, including the Lacedaemonian army, was required for a particular operation. We hear of levies of 4,000, 6,000 and 10,000.[2] When they themselves sent out a part of their forces only they required a proportion from their allies.[3] This system must have caused difficulties in calculating individual contingents; so all the cities were now divided into ten groups. The Lacedaemonians themselves formed one, and so did the Eleans, the Achaeans, the Acarnanians, and the Thracian cities. The Arcadians formed two groups, the Corinthians with the Megarians another, the Phocians and Locrians another, while one was composed of the Sicyonians, Phliasians and the Argolic cities. Each group supplied an equal contingent, a hoplite being reckoned as equal to two light-armed, and a cavalryman to four hoplites.[4]

Next spring (376) Agesilaus again ravaged Boeotia, and again by a feint penetrated the stockade and ravaged the plain of Thebes. The Thebans were by now very short of corn, and tried to import ten talents worth from Pagasae in Thessaly. Alcetas,

[1] Diod. XV. 28, 30.
[2] Xen. Hell. III. i. 4, iv. 2, V. ii. 20.
[3] Xen. Hell. IV. vi. 3, VI. i. 1.
[4] Diod. XV. 31.

the Spartan commander at Hestiaea, intercepted the ships and brought them into the port of Oreus, but the crews, whom he imprisoned in the acropolis, broke out and raised the city in revolt. So the Thebans got their corn and a new ally.[1]

Next spring (375) Agesilaus was ill and Cleombrotus was put in command. He was unable to force the passes of Cithaeron against Theban and Athenian resistance and retired. A conference of the Peloponnesian League was then held, in which the others accused the Spartans of lack of initiative and suggested that a fleet be built in order to blockade Athens and transport the army by sea to Boeotia. Sixty ships were accordingly manned, and Pollis, the Spartan admiral, basing himself on Aegina, Ceos and Andros, tried to intercept the cornships sailing into Athens. The Athenians, however, manned a larger fleet of over 80 ships, and under the command of Chabrias inflicted a sharp defeat on the Spartans near Naxos, sinking 24 ships and capturing 8 at a loss of 18 Athenian ships, whose crews were all saved.[2]

The Thebans, fearing another invasion, urged the Athenians to make a diversion, and the latter responded by sending Timotheus round the Peloponnese with 60 ships. He won over Corcyra to the Athenian alliance, and the Spartans sent their admiral Nicolochus with 55 ships to resist him. He engaged Timotheus and was defeated. Timotheus with Corcyraean aid built up his fleet to over 70 ships but found great difficulty in paying his men.[3]

Meanwhile the Thebans, freed from Spartan interference, made renewed attacks on the other Boeotian cities, and having reduced them went on to invade Phocis. The Spartans decided that they could not ignore this move, and sent Cleandridas with four *morae* and a partial levy of allies to Phocis by sea. They were about this time approached by Polydamas, the leader of the Thessalian city of Pharsalus, who described to them the growing power of Jason, the leader of another Thessalian city, Pherae, and represented

[1] Xen. *Hell.* V. iv. 47–57.   [2] Xen. *Hell.* V. iv. 58–61; Diod. XV. 34–5.
[3] Xen. *Hell.* V. iv. 62–6.

that if Jason was allowed to make himself master of Thessaly, as he seemed likely to do, he would be a serious threat to Sparta. The Spartans, however, thought that they were too heavily involved by their other commitments, and decided to take no action.[1]

The Athenians were by this time getting war weary. They were subject to blockade from Aegina, were taxing themselves heavily to maintain a large fleet, and were moreover not too pleased with the way in which the Thebans were increasing their power at the expense of old Athenian allies like the Phocians. They therefore and the Spartans responded to an initiative from King Artaxerxes, who proposed a general peace for reasons of his own. He was planning to reduce Acoris, the rebel king of Egypt, and wanted to raise Greek mercenaries, who would be more plentiful and cheaper if Greece were at peace. Peace was signed between Sparta and Athens and their respective allies, on condition that all cities should be autonomous and ungarrisoned, but the Thebans refused to come in (374).[2]

The peace was scarcely signed before it was broken. Instructions were sent to Timotheus to sail home, but on the way he gave assistance to the democratic exiles of Zacynthus, and the Zacynthian government complained to Sparta. The Spartans promptly manned a fleet of 60 ships, provided by themselves, Corinth, Leucas, Ambracia, Elis, Achaea and the Argolic cities and Zacynthus, and placed it under the command of Mnasippus, providing him also with 1,500 mercenaries. He reduced the Corcyraeans to great straits, and they appealed to Athens, which sent 600 peltasts by land to support them, and later a fleet of 70 ships under Iphicrates. Dionysius, tyrant of Syracuse, sent 10 ships to support the Spartans, but Iphicrates intercepted them, and successfully relieved Corcyra and also reduced Cephallenia.[3]

On the initiative of Artaxerxes another peace conference was held (371). Despite their successes the Athenians were desperately

---

[1] Xen. *Hell.* VI. i.   [2] Xen. *Hell.* VI. ii. 1; Diod. XV. 38.
[3] Xen. *Hell.* VI. ii. 2–38.

short of money, and were even more alienated from the Thebans, who had expelled their old allies, the Plataeans, from their city, and were threatening Thespiae. After long discussions a general peace was agreed on the terms that all cities should be autonomous, and all harmosts withdrawn, and armies and navies disbanded. If any city infringed the peace, any city which wished could assist the victim, but no city was obliged to do so. The Spartans signed on behalf of their allies, the Athenians and their allies signed individually, and the Thebans signed. Next day they demanded that their signature should be altered from 'the Thebans' to 'the Boeotians'. Agesilaus refused to accept the change and the Athenians supported him.[1]

Thebes was now isolated. Cleombrotus, who was in Phocis with four *morae*, asked the authorities at home for instructions. At the Spartan assembly, Prothous urged that his army should be demobilized like the rest according to the terms of the peace, and that then, if any city infringed the autonomy of any other, common action should be taken. The assembly rejected this plea, and ordered Cleombrotus to move forthwith on Thebes, unless she freed the Boeotian cities. He obeyed and encamped at Leuctra in Thespian territory. Cleombrotus was afraid of incurring censure at home if he failed to fight, and the Thebans feared that if they did not fight the Boeotian cities would desert them. In the battle which ensued the Spartans were well and truly beaten, losing 400 Spartiates.[2]

[1] Xen. *Hell.* VI. iii; Diod. XV. 50, cf. 46.   [2] Xen. *Hell.* VI. iv. 2–15, cf. VI. i. 1.

XXII

MESSENE AND MEGALOPOLIS

THE Spartans were celebrating the Gymnopaedia when the news came. The ephors notified the relations of the dead, but forbade mourning. The survivors of Leuctra should according to Spartan custom have been subjected to sundry marks of disgrace and political disabilities, but at this crisis the ephors hesitated to deal severely with so large a number of citizens, and on Agesilaus' advice suspended the law.[1] To meet the military situation they ordered a levy of the two remaining *morae* up to the age of 59. They also summoned their allies, and received contingents from Tegea, the villages of Mantinea, Corinth, Sicyon, Phlius, the Achaeans and some other cities. They also manned a fleet from the Lacedaemonians, Corinthians and Sicyonians. As Agesilaus was unwell, his son Archidamus was put in command and marched to the Isthmus.[2]

The Thebans forthwith announced their victory to the Athenians and asked for their aid. Their envoys received a chilly reception and no aid was offered. They also sent to their ally Jason of Pherae for aid, suggesting that by a combined attack they should destroy the Lacedaemonian army. He responded promptly, but advised caution, and arranged a truce under which the defeated army was allowed to go home unmolested. It joined Archidamus' army at Corinth and then the whole force was disbanded.[3]

The Spartiate casualties at Leuctra were a heavy blow. Xenophon[4] tells us that there were 700 Spartiates of the age classes from 20 to 54 in the four *morae* that fought at Leuctra, and there must therefore have been about 350 of the same age classes in the other

---

[1] Plut. *Ages*. 30.
[2] Xen. *Hell*. VI. iv. 16–8.
[3] Xen. *Hell*. VI. iv. 19–26.
[4] *Hell*. VI. iv. 15, cf. 17.

two *morae*. To this total of 1,050 must be added the men over 54, but they cannot have numbered much over 300 and were of little military value. Of this total 400, about a third of the men of military age, had been killed. It must, however, be remembered that for a long while past the Spartiates had been a minority in the Lacedaemonian army, which consisted mainly of Perioeci. Of the whole Lacedaemonian force 1,000 had perished, a smaller proportion of the total. Given a healthy birth rate these losses could have been repaired in a generation.

Much more serious was the blow to Spartan prestige. For the first time for centuries a Lacedaemonian army had been decisively defeated in fair fight. The Spartans had lost their reputation for invincibility, and all their many enemies took courage.

The Athenians seized the opportunity to make a big diplomatic initiative. They called a congress of all signatories of the King's Peace and proposed that they should swear the following oath: 'I will abide by the truce which the King sent down and the decrees of the Athenians and their allies. If anyone attacks any city which has sworn this oath, I will assist with all my power.' This attempt to steal from Sparta not only her position as arbiter of the King's Peace, but also her own league, met with surprising success. The Eleans, it is true, refused to sign because the Triphylian cities taken from them by Sparta were recognized as autonomous, but all the others took the oath. It had, however, little practical effect; some cities remained loyal to Sparta and those that did not played for their own hand.[1]

The next trouble for Sparta was in the Peloponnese. It began in Arcadia. The Mantinean people determined to unite in their old city and rebuild its walls. Agesilaus remonstrated but dared not attempt force, and the walls were rebuilt with aid in money and men from the Eleans and from other Arcadian communities. At Tegea the dominant pro-Spartan group led by Stasippus were opposed by a popular group led by Callibius and Proxenus. The

[1] Xen. *Hell.* VI. v. 1–3.

latter were defeated in the council and appealed to the people, taking up arms. Stasippus' group counter-attacked, killed some of his opponents, including Proxenus, and drove the rest from the city. Callibius' party appealed to the Mantineans, who marched against Tegea. The gates were flung open and Stasippus' group were some of them executed, while others, numbering about 800, fled to Sparta.[1]

Both Callibius at Tegea and the leading democratic politician at Mantinea, Lycomedes, planned an Arcadian federation. There was to be a general assembly of all Arcadians (or perhaps all Arcadian hoplites), styled the Ten Thousand, which controlled foreign policy and military affairs, a council whose members were appointed by the several cities and other communities in rough proportion to their importance, a general and a federal *corps d'élite*, called the Eparitoi, numbering five thousand and paid by the contributions of the cities. The idea was ambitious, but not very practical, for Arcadia was not much more than a geographical expression, and though the Arcadians had a common dialect and some common cults, and prided themselves on being the original inhabitants of the Peloponnese, unlike their Elean and Dorian neighbours, the various Arcadian communities were riven by local rivalries.[2]

It was probably also at this date that a plan was formed of founding a great city, Megalopolis, in south-western Arcadia; Pausanias[3] dates the foundation in the year 371–370, and Diodorus'[4] date of 368 may be that of the completion of the design. The inhabitants of this area had hitherto lived in villages, some 40 in number, grouped in tribal confederations, the Maenalians, Parrhasians, Eutresians, Aegytians, Cinurians.[5] This state of affairs was convenient to Sparta, since it meant that no fortified city barred the way to her armies into Arcadia should Tegea and Mantinea

[1] Xen. *Hell.* VI. v. 3–10.
[2] Diod. XV. 59; Tod. *Greek Hist. Inscr.* 132; Xen. *Hell.* VI. v. 6; cf. Diod. XV, 62.2, 67.2; Xen. *Hell.* VII. iv. 33, 36 ff. for the Eparitoi. The 50 *damiorgoi* of Tod, 132, are probably not the council but its presiding committee, who also presided in the assembly.
[3] VIII. xxvii. 8.   [4] XV. 72.   [5] Diod. XV. 72; Paus. VIII. xxvii. 3–4.

be hostile, and the Spartans had no doubt discouraged any movement towards unity. Now there was, or shortly would be, a powerful fortress hemming them in.

Tegea, Mantinea and the south-western Arcadians favoured the federation. Other Arcadian cities resisted the proposal; the people of Orchomenus were old enemies of the Mantineans and admitted a mercenary garrison sent from Corinth, and the Heraeans and Lepreates were loyal to Sparta. The Spartans decided to intervene, and appointed Agesilaus to the command. He occupied Eutaea, which had joined the Arcadian league and had sent all its fighting men to Asea, where the federal army was assembling. Lycomedes of Mantinea, general of the Arcadian league, meanwhile attacked Orchomenus at the head of the Eparitoi, and defeated the mercenaries and killed their leader. Agesilaus marched on Mantinea, and ravaged its territory, but he did not dare to attack the Arcadian army, which was supported by the Argives and Eleans. The enemy also refused to attack, for they had asked for Athenian aid and on the latter's refusal had applied to Thebes and were expecting the arrival of the Theban army. Agesilaus was forced to retreat to Sparta having achieved nothing.[1]

The Thebans now arrived with the other Boeotians and their new allies the Phocians, the Euboeans, the Locrians, the Acarnanians, the Heracleots, the Malians, and some Thessalian cavalry and peltasts. Finding the enemy gone they at first wished to return home, but were persuaded by the Arcadians, Eleans and Argives to invade Laconia itself: they were encouraged by some Perioeci, who declared that they would revolt if Laconia were invaded.[2]

The allies invaded Laconia in four columns by different routes. The Arcadians had to overcome the garrison of Oeon in the Sciritis, and the Argives also met with resistance, but the Thebans and the Eleans marched in unopposed. The four columns reunited at Sellasia and marched down the left bank of the Eurotas. To

---

[1] Xen. *Hell.* VI. v. 10–22; Diod. XV. 62.   [2] Xen. *Hell.* VI. v. 23–5.

face this menace the Spartans offered their freedom to Helot volunteers and enrolled as many as 6,000. They were at first rather nervous of the reliability of this large force, but gathered confidence when they were reinforced by the mercenaries from Orchomenus and by contingents from their still faithful allies, Corinth, Phlius, Epidaurus, Troezen, Hermione, Halieis, Sicyon and Pellene. These contingents had found great difficulty in making their way to Sparta. They had had to take ship in the Argolid, and sail in relays—presumably owing to shortage of shipping—to the Perioecic town of Prasiae on the east coast of Laconia and thence make their way across the mountains.[1] The Theban army crossed the river opposite Amyclae, and ravaged the Spartan territory, but did not venture to attack the city. Some Perioeci joined them, but only a few individuals, it would seem, and Gytheum withstood a three days' assault.[2]

The Theban general, Epaminondas, now withdrew, but before he left the Peloponnese he persuaded the Arcadians and their allies to found the city of Messene at the foot of Mount Ithome, concentrating in it the local population, and recalling to it the bodies of Messenian exiles in Sicily, Italy and Cyrenaica.[3] Thus after 230 years the Messenians became independent once more, and Sparta lost nearly half her territory. It is not certain how far Messenian territory extended. To the south-west on the peninsula of Cape Acritas the Perioecic cities of Asine and Methone, whose inhabitants were not Messenians,[4] remained loyal to Sparta.[5] So also did the Perioecic towns on the peninsula of Taenarum, including those on its western slopes. But Sparta also lost territory on her northern frontier. The Sciritae, for so long a *corps d'élite* in the Lacedaemonian army, seem to have thrown in their lot with their Arcadian kinsmen: at any rate Archidamus a few years later ravaged 'as much of Arcadia and the Sciritis as he could'.[6] Even Sellasia was for some time in Arcadian hands.[7]

[1] Xen. *Hell*. VI. v. 26–9; VII. ii. 2–3.   [2] Xen. *Hell*. VI. v. 25–32; Diod. XV. 64–5.
[3] Diod. XV. 66; Paus. IV. xxvi. 5, xxvii. 11.   [4] Paus. IV. xiv. 3, xxiv. 4, xxxiv. 9.
[5] Scylax 46; Xen. *Hell*. VII. i. 25; cf. Paus. IV. xxvii. 8.
[6] Xen. *Hell*. VII. iv. 21.   [7] Xen. *Hell*. VII. iv. 12.

The Spartans had indeed been humbled, but their effective strength had not been greatly reduced. The Messenian Helots had always been more of a liability than an asset, and the independent state of Messene proved to be less of a threat than the discontented Helots had been. On the other hand the invasion had proved the loyalty of the Laconian Helots and of the Perioeci, who had with very few exceptions stood by Sparta in the hour of danger. The evidence on this point is contradictory. In one passage Xenophon[1] declares that Phlius remained loyal when the Spartans 'had been beaten at the battle of Leuctra, and many Perioeci had revolted, and all the Helots had revolted and moreover their allies except for a very few'. But this is a very rhetorical passage, designed to set the loyalty of Phlius in relief, and in the actual narrative we only have that 'there were some of the Perioeci who joined in the attack and marched with the Thebans' against Gytheum, which they failed to take.[2] Plutarch too in his life of Agesilaus[3] speaks only of individual desertions, and of one body of 200 men, who occupied a position without orders, but submitted when Agesilaus recalled them; he executed the fifteen ringleaders the following night. Another conspiracy is reported, in which Spartiates had a part; it was nipped in the bud and the participants executed without trial despite their status.[4] Sparta, moreover, still had some allies of proven loyalty, and in her fallen fortunes she won the friendship of her old enemy Athens. Spartan envoys were sent to Athens and enlarged on the occasions on which they had worked together and given each other mutual aid. What influenced the Athenians more, perhaps, was their longstanding hatred of Thebes, which had revived with the growth of Theban power. At any rate a treaty was signed and Iphicrates invaded Arcadia, but perhaps deliberately failed to close the Isthmus to the returning Theban army.[5]

The loss of Messenia must have yet further reduced the number of Spartiates, for the old rule that a Spartiate lost his citizen rights

[1] *Hell.* VII. ii. 2.   [2] Xen. *Hell.* VI. v. 32.   [3] Plut. *Ages.* 32.
[4] Plut. *Ages.* 32; Polyaenus, II. i. 14; Aelian, *Var. Hist.* xiv. 27.
[5] Xen. *Hell.*, VI. v. 33–52.

if he failed to pay his mess bill was not abrogated, and some Spartiates must have depended on Messenian estates. The Spartiate body had, however, already sunk to about 1,300 before Leuctra, and was still about 1,000 in Aristotle's[1] day; so the loss cannot have been serious. The decline in Spartiate numbers was of long standing and seems to have been due to deliberate family restriction over the generations. It was certainly not due to battle casualties, for the Spartan army was so well disciplined and so generally victorious that casualties were few. Thermopylae, Pylos, Lechaeum and Leuctra were very exceptional.

There is no reason to think that the law or custom of inheritance in Sparta differed from those prevalent in most Greek cities. Daughters received dowries: according to Aristotle[2] large dowries were given, 'and yet it would have been better that none or small and moderate ones should have been ordained'. If there were several sons all inherited, apparently in equal shares. This is implied by Aristotle's[3] criticism of the law which gave exemption from military service to the father of three sons and complete immunity to the father of four. 'And yet it is obvious that if there are many, and the land is divided in this way, many must become poor.' Xenophon[4] also remarks that Spartiate husbands, when they allowed their wives to bear children by other men, were glad 'to receive brothers for their sons, who share in their family and increase their power, but make no claim to the property'. If there were no sons the father might with the approval of the kings adopt a son.[5] Otherwise his daughter or daughters became his heiress or heiresses and he might betroth her or them to anyone he wished.[6] If he died before doing so, the king according to Herodotus disposed of the heiress, but in Aristotle's day the father's heir, even if he died without a will, could give the heiress to anyone he wished—or presumably marry her himself.[7]

[1] *Pol.* II. ix. 16, 1270a.   [2] *Pol.* II. ix. 15, 1270a.   [3] *Pol.* II. ix. 18–19, 1270b.
[4] *Resp. Lac.* i. 9.   [5] Herod. VI. 57.   [6] Arist. *Pol.* II. ix. 15. 1270a.
[7] Herod. VI. 57, Arist. *Pol.* II. ix. 15. 1270a.

Some poor and impoverished Spartiates doubtless had large families, and their sons, when they divided the inheritance, were too poor to maintain their contributions to the *pheiditia* and became Inferiors. Provident Spartiates probably restricted themselves to one son, who inherited the undivided estate. But sometimes the son died without issue, and the estate was then left to a friend, who might be adopted, or passed to a daughter. The latter case seems to have been more frequent; in Aristotle's day two-fifths of the land was owned by women: Spartan women, or at any rate widows, seem to have controlled their own fortunes.[1] In any case the recipient of the land, the adopted heir, legatee or son-in-law, would usually mostly be a landowner on his own account, and land thus accumulated in the hands of a diminishing group of wealthy men.

Xenophon[2] and Plutarch[3] attribute the decline of Sparta to the influx of wealth after the fall of Athens and the consequent growth of luxury. But this, by introducing high standards of living, mainly accentuated existing trends, making Spartans still more unwilling to divide their inheritance between several sons. Already in the fifth century there were glaring contrasts in wealth between Spartiates. Lysander, a Heraclid, was so poor that he received his training as a Mothax,[4] whereas Lichas not only won the chariot race at the Olympia in 420,[5] but was famous throughout Greece for the lavish entertainment he gave to all strangers at the Gymnopaedia.[6] Plutarch also attached much importance to the *rhetra* of Epitadeus, which he apparently dated to the early fourth century.[7] Epitadeus, having quarrelled with his son, passed a bill making it legal for a Spartan to give or bequeath his land to anyone he wished, even to the exclusion of a son. But it is difficult to believe that many Spartiates disinherited their sons in favour of wealthy friends.

[1] Anst. *Pol.* II. ix. 15, 1270a. Cf. the large fortunes of Cynisca, daughter of Archidamus, who won the chariot race at Olympia, Paus. III. viii. 1–2, xv. i, V. xii. 5, VI. i. 6, and of Agesistrata and Archidamia, the mother and grandmother of Agis IV, Plut. *Agis*, 4.
[2] *Resp. Lac.* xiv.   [3] *Lyc.* 30, *Agis*, 5.   [4] See pp. 37-8.   [5] Thuc. V. 50.
[6] Xen. *Mem.* I. ii. 61; Plut. *Cimon*, 10.   [7] Plut. *Agis*, 5.

Numbers had early begun to decline. Reports that the Spartiates once numbered 10,000 or 9,000[1] need not be taken seriously. Demaratus told Xerxes that the Spartans numbered 8,000,[2] but this is probably an exaggeration, for at Plataea they turned out only 5,000 men.[3] We unfortunately have no further figures until the 1,300 of the year of Leuctra (371), but numbers must have dropped very sharply by the year of Mantinea (418) when the total levy of Spartiates and Perioeci came only to 6,000.[4]

The dwindling number of Spartiates meant that the Lacedaemonian state became an increasingly narrow oligarchy, with fewer and fewer full citizens ruling over a subject population of Inferiors, Perioeci, Neodamodeis and Helots. But so long as the Perioeci and the Laconian Helots remained loyal, the military strength of Sparta was not greatly reduced by the decline in Spartiate numbers. The reduction of Helot numbers by the refoundation of Messene might be regarded as a gain, since it reduced the gross disproportion between rulers and subjects.

---

[1] Arist. *Pol.* II. ix. 17, 1270a; Plut. *Lyc.* 8, 16.   [2] Herod. VII. 234.
[3] Herod. IX. 28.   [4] See p. 62.

XXIII

THE THEBAN SUPREMACY

THE next year (369) the Athenians, the Spartans and their still faithful allies, the Megarians, Corinthians, Pellenians, Phliasians, Sicyonians, Epidaurians, and the other cities of the Argolid, tried to block the Isthmus against the Thebans, building a stockade across it. Epaminondas, however, by attacking all along the line simultaneously at the time when the allies were changing watch, but pressing his attack on the Lacedaemonian sector, succeeded in breaking through. He ravaged the territories of Epidaurus, Troezen and other cities, and succeeded in winning over Sicyon and installing in it a Theban commander and garrison. He also appears to have won over Pellene, but an attack on Corinth was beaten off with loss by the Athenian general Chabrias. Later in the year twenty triremes, sent by Dionysius, arrived from Syracuse, and with them 2,000 Gallic and Spanish mercenaries, with pay for five months. When the Theban army had retired these defeated the Sicyonians but failed to recapture the town, and then sailed home.[1]

Next year the Thebans were not invited to invade the Peloponnese. Lycomedes of Mantinea, declaring that the Arcadians were the best soldiers in Greece, that they were always in demand as mercenaries, and that Spartans had never invaded Athens without Arcadian aid, or the Thebans invaded Laconia, urged his countrymen to take an independent line instead of leaning on foreign support. Following his advice the Arcadians campaigned on their own, relieving the Argives, who had attacked Epidaurus, and had in turn been cut off and blockaded by Chabrias the Athenian;

[1] Xen. *Hell*. VII. i. 15–22, cf. VII. ii. 11; Diod. XV. 68–70.

and attacking Asine, a Perioecic town south-west of Messenia, still loyal to Sparta, killing a Spartan polemarch who was defending it, and destroying its suburbs. Lycomedes also asserted Arcadian claims over the Triphylian and neighbouring cities which had been taken by Sparta from Elis in 398, resisting the attempts of Elis to recover them.[1]

In the same year the Persian satrap Ariobarzanes sent Philiscus of Abydos with a large sum of money to try to negotiate a general truce. He called a conference at Delphi, but the Spartans refused to acknowledge the independence of Messene, and the Thebans insisted upon it, so that a deadlock ensued. Philiscus collected 2,000 mercenaries and left them with their pay to serve on the Spartan side.[2]

In the following year (367) Dionysius of Syracuse sent a smaller force of mercenaries to assist Sparta. With their and his own troops Archidamus recaptured Caryae and ravaged the territory of the Parrhasians. The other Arcadians and the Argives came to their support, and at this juncture Cissidas, the commander of Dionysius' mercenaries, declared that the time for his return had come and marched off towards Sparta. However, when the Messenians harried his route, he was forced to ask Archidamus for aid. Archidamus went to help him, but in the territory of the Eutresians the Spartans and the mercenaries were attacked by the Argives and Arcadians. Archidamus won a brilliant victory without the loss of a single Lacedaemonian. The news of this 'tearless victory' greatly raised morale at Sparta.[3]

In the same year the Thebans, led by Epaminondas, invaded the Peloponnese with the object of bringing the Achaean cities, which were still loyal to Sparta, over to the Theban side as a counterweight to the over-independent Arcadians. Oneion, the key fortress of the Isthmus, was held by an Athenian general and a Spartan commander with a force of mercenaries, but Epaminondas got the Argive general Peisias to surprise it, and was thus

---

[1] Xen. Hell. VII. i. 23–6.   [2] Xen. Hell. VII. i. 27; Diod. XV. 70.
[3] Xen. Hell. VII. i. 28–32; Diod. XV. 72.

able to march into the Peloponnese. The aristocratic governments of the Achaean cities agreed to join the Theban side, and Epaminondas accordingly allowed them to remain in power. On his return home, however, his political opponents at Thebes, backed by the Arcadians, accused him of playing into Spartan hands, and the Thebans sent harmosts to the Achaean cities, who expelled the aristocrats and established democratic governments. The Achaean aristocrats recovered the cities as soon as the Thebans were gone, and naturally were henceforth more loyal than ever to Sparta.[1] The only other fruit of the expedition was that the Achaeans lost Naupactus and Calydon, on the north of the gulf of Corinth.[2]

In Sicyon too the old aristocratic government had been left in power when the city accepted Theban suzerainty. An ambitious Sicyonian politician, Euphron, now represented to the Arcadians and Argives that Sicyon would be better secured if a democracy were established. With their support he proclaimed a democracy and was elected general with five colleagues. Having secured the support of the mercenary garrison he expelled the pro-Spartan aristocrats, and, having liquidated his colleagues, made himself tyrant.[3]

The Thebans in the meanwhile opened negotiations with the Persian king with the object of imposing on Greece a general peace in accord with their ambitions. They sent Pelopidas up to Susa, and the Arcadians Antiochus and the Eleans Archidamus. They found a Spartan ambassador, Euthycles, already there and the Athenians also decided to send two envoys, Timagoras and Leon. Pelopidas made a speech dwelling on the old friendship of Thebes to Persia and her present military power. He was asked what terms he proposed, and he answered that Messene should be independent of Sparta, and the Athenians should put their fleet into dock. The Athenian Leon remarked: 'It is time for you,

[1] Xen. *Hell*. VII. i. 41–3.   [2] Diod. XV. 75.   [3] Xen. *Hell*. VII. i. 44–6.

Athenians, it seems, to look for another friend than the King', and the Persian king ordered that a note be added that 'if the Athenians find a juster proposal than this, they should come and inform the King'. It would also appear that the proposed peace recognized the dependence of the Triphylians on Elis, for the Arcadian delegate was highly displeased, and reported to the Ten Thousand that the Persian king had plenty of bakers and cooks and waiters and footmen, but no fighting men capable of freeing the Greeks.[1]

The Thebans now summoned a congress of all Greek cities, and the Persian delegate produced the treaty sealed with the royal seal and read it. The Thebans demanded that all the delegates should swear, but they replied that they had been summoned to hear the terms not to swear to them. Lycomedes the Arcadian went further and demanded that future congresses should not always meet in Thebes, but wherever the war was. The congress broke up and the Thebans sent envoys to the several cities, hoping that they would sign for fear of being isolated as enemies of Thebes and Persia. However, the Corinthians refused to sign, and the other cities did likewise.[2]

These abortive negotiations seem to have occupied the years 367–366. There were no major military operations in 366 or 365. The Theban commander of Sicyon with his mercenaries, and Euphron, the tyrant of Sicyon, with his, which numbered 2,000, and the citizen levies of Sicyon and Pellene, attacked the city of Phlius, which was still stubbornly loyal to Sparta, but without success, and the Athenian general Chares came to the support of Phlius, and helped to provison it. Then the Arcadian federal general, Aeneas of Stymphalus, intervened; he recalled the men that Euphron had exiled and summoned an assembly of them and of the upper class citizens. Euphron, fearing for his life, marched to the port of Sicyon and surrendered it to the

[1] Xen. *Hell.* VII. i. 33–8.   [2] Xen. *Hell.* VII. i. 39–40.

Spartans. Later Euphron hired mercenaries at Athens, and taking advantage of civil dissensions at Sicyon seized the city. As, however, the Theban commander still held the acropolis, he went to Thebes hoping to win Theban support by changing sides. He was, however, murdered in Thebes by Sicyonian exiles. These exiles claimed that they had been justified in killing a tyrant and traitor and the Thebans acquitted them. Sicyon then returned to the Theban alliance.[1]

Lycomedes the Arcadian, looking round for an ally less aggressive than Thebes, approached Athens. This was a rather odd move, as Athens was the ally of Sparta, Arcadia's chief enemy, but Lycomedes was aware that the Athenians were dissatisfied with the conduct of their allies, who gave them no assistance against Thebes; and on the other hand the Athenians reflected that if they alienated Arcadia from Thebes they would be doing a good turn to Sparta. Lycomedes was killed by Arcadian exiles on his return journey, but the alliance was formed none the less.[2]

To make communications between Athens and Arcadia more secure the Athenians, who were already maintaining garrisons in a number of Corinthian frontier fortresses, decided to occupy Corinth. But the Corinthians, getting wind of this, sent troops to all the frontier forts and ordered the Athenians to withdraw. Chares, who sailed into the Corinthian port of Cenchreae at this juncture, was also politely asked to leave, and Corinth thus freed herself from the danger of Athenian control.[3]

The Corinthians hired mercenaries to stiffen their army, but it was clearly hopeless to attempt to carry on the war with not only Arcadia and Argos but also Athens against them, and they appealed to Thebes to ask if offers of peace would be favourably received. On getting an affirmative answer they asked if they might consult their allies and gain their assent. They then went to Sparta, and declared that they were willing to carry on the

[1] Xen. *Hell.* VII. ii. 11–iii. 12. [2] Xen. *Hell.* VII. iv. 2–3.
[3] Xen. *Hell.* VII. iv. 4–6.

142

war if the Spartans could offer any hope of success, but that as the situation was hopeless they wished to make peace with the Thebans, and urged the Spartans to do likewise. If the Spartans wished to carry on the war, they asked leave to make a separate peace. The Spartans replied that they would carry on the war, but raised no objection to the Corinthians or their other allies making peace. The Corinthians accordingly made peace with Thebes; they refused a proffered alliance, however, declaring that peace was all they wanted. Phlius, Epidaurus and, it would seem, other Spartan allies in the area made peace on the same terms.[1]

The ancient alliance of Sparta and Corinth was thus amicably dissolved and the Peloponnesian League virtually ceased to exist. The only allies which Sparta still kept in the Peloponnese were the Achaeans: Pellene, which had deserted to the Thebans, rejoined the Achaean league about this time. But at the same time dissensions were breaking out between her former allies, the Arcadians and the Eleans, and the fragile unity of Arcadia began to crack. The Eleans occupied Lasion, one of their former subject cities, now a member of the Arcadian league. A battle ensued in which the Eleans were defeated. The Arcadians proceeded to occupy Olympia and the surrounding territory, and broke into the city of Elis itself. In Elis, as in most cities, there was a democratic party and an aristocratic party. The latter were in power, and the former welcomed the Arcadians. An attack on the acropolis failed, however, and the beaten democrats, to the number of about 400, were expelled from the city, and established at Pylos, a fortified post in Elean territory, where they were joined by other democratic exiles. The Achaeans came in on the Elean side.[2]

The Spartans next sent a contingent to support the Eleans, but the Arcadians won a victory over their combined forces. Archidamus tried, at the request of Elis, to make a diversion, and

---

[1] Xen. *Hell.* VII. iv. 6–11; cf. Isocrates, VI. 91.   [2] Xen. *Hell.* VII. iv. 12–8.

captured the Arcadian city of Cromnus, and garrisoned it with three *lochoi*: the Arcadians proceeded to blockade it and Archidamus again invaded Arcadia and ravaged the country. He tried to relieve Cromnus but was beaten off with loss, about thirty Spartans being killed and he himself wounded.[1]

Meanwhile the Eleans attacked and destroyed Pylos, slaughtering the exiles. The Spartans again tried to raise the siege of Cromnus, which was being pressed not only by the Arcadians but by their allies the Argives, the Messenians, and some Theban troops. The Spartans succeeded in evacuating most of their troops: but over a hundred Spartans and Perioeci were captured.[2]

The Arcadians, having recaptured Cromnus, went to Olympia, where they began to celebrate the festival (364) in the name of the Pisatae, the alleged primitive owners of the shrine. The Eleans with the Achaeans attacked them, but 2,000 Argive infantry and 400 Athenian horse came to their support. The Eleans at first defeated their opponents and penetrated into the sanctuary, but ultimately had to retire.[3]

The Arcadian league was by now finding difficulty in paying the Eparitoi, and proceeded to draw upon the sacred funds of Olympia. This measure caused dissensions in the league, and the Mantineans refused to join in it, but sent their contribution from their own resources. The federal authorities declared that the Mantineans were sabotaging the league and summoned their leaders before the Ten Thousand. They refused to appear and were condemned in absence, and the Eparitoi were sent to arrest them. The Mantineans closed their gates and refused to admit the Eparitoi, and other Arcadians began to have qualms about the sacred funds, and the Ten Thousand decided to draw on them no longer. The result was the poorer Eparitoi had to leave the service, and only the richer members carried on. The federal magistrates, fearing that the pro-Spartan elements in Arcadia might gain control, sent to Thebes to ask for aid. The opposing

[1] Xen. *Hell.* VII. iv. 19–25.   [2] Xen. *Hell.* VII. iv. 26–7.
[3] Xen. *Hell.* VII. 28–32.

party, however, persuaded the Ten Thousand to conclude a truce with Elis.[1]

Chaos followed. The local Boeotian commander had sworn to the truce, but now he and the pro-Theban federal officers closed the gates of Tegea with the aid of the 300 Boeotians present and their sympathizers among the Eparitoi, and tried to arrest the opposition, who were in camp outside the city. They crammed the prison and the public buildings with prisoners, but many escaped, including most of the Mantineans, who fled to Mantinea. The Mantineans put themselves in a state of defence and demanded that such Mantineans as had been arrested should be released and that illegal arrests and executions should be stayed until a proper trial could be held; they promised in this case that they would produce the accused before the federal court. The Theban commander was alarmed and released the Mantinean prisoners, and excused his previous action on the plea that he had thought that the city was being betrayed to the Spartans. The opposition sent to Thebes to accuse him, but Epaminondas declared that his action in making the arrests had been correct, and that the peace with Elis was a treacherous breach of treaty.[2]

The Mantineans now came out openly on the Spartan side, joining with the Eleans and Achaeans in denouncing the intervention of Thebes in the Peloponnese. They sent to Athens for aid, and the Eparitoi, by now an aristocratic corps, appealed to the Spartans. Meanwhile Epaminondas marched with the Boeotians, the Euboeans and some Thessalians, wishing to join his allies in the Peloponnese, the Argives, the Messenians and the Arcadian cities of Tegea, Megalopolis, Asea and Pallantium. He paused at Nemea, hoping to catch the Athenians on their march south, but the Athenians did not appear. During his delay his opponents mustered at Mantinea. Epaminondas then moved to Tegea, and Agesilaus started for Mantinea. When he had reached Pellene, Epaminondas marched on Sparta, which was denuded of all its

[1] Xen. *Hell*. VII. iv. 33–5.   [2] Xen. *Hell*. VII. iv. 36–40.

fighting men. Agesilaus, however, received news of this move just in time and marched back. Even so the city was weakly held, for all the cavalry and the mercenaries and 3 of the 12 *lochi* were in Arcadia. But, having failed to achieve his surprise Epaminondas, though he actually penetrated into the city, did not press his attack. Instead he returned to Tegea, and from there sent on his cavalry to Mantinea, hoping to take the Mantineans unawares. But this was frustrated also, for the Athenian cavalry arrived in the nick of time and in a spirited action beat the Boeotians off.[1]

A full scale battle was now inevitable. The two great armies met at Mantinea and Epaminondas won the victory but was himself killed.[2]

[1] Xen. *Hell.* VII. v. 1–17.   [2] Xen. *Hell.* VII. v. 18–27; Diod. XV. 84–7.

XXIV

SPARTA IN ECLIPSE

A FTER the second battle of Mantinea the Greek cities signed a common peace: only Sparta refused to come in because Messene was recognized.[1] Agesilaus took service under the Egyptian rebel king Tachos, thereby earning 230 talents—which was no doubt the object of the exercise.[2] He died in Libya. So died King Agesilaus, the idol of Xenophon, who not only devoted a disproportionate amount of his Hellenica to his exploits, but wrote a encomiastic biography of him. He held the reins of power in Sparta throughout his long reign, meeting with very little effective opposition. This was partly because he was an able general, who always won his battles and who endeared himself to his men by his care for their welfare.[3] But he was also politically astute, exploiting his natural *bonhomie* to conciliate the elders and the successive boards of ephors.[4] He was, moreover, lucky in his colleagues. Agesipolis I was still a child when Agesilaus succeeded, and still quite young when he died. According to Diodorus,[5] 'Agesipolis was a lover of peace and justice, and highly intelligent, and maintained that oaths should be observed, and that the Greeks ought not to be enslaved contrary to the Common Peace. For he declared that Sparta was dishonoured in having surrendered the Greeks in Asia to the Persians, while she herself plotted against the cities of Greece which she had sworn in the common treaty not to enslave but to maintain autonomous.' If these were Agesipolis' sentiments he seems to have concealed them very well, for he lived on terms of great intimacy with

---

[1] Diod. XV. 89; Plut. *Ages.* 35; Polyb. IV. 33.
[2] Plut. *Ages.* 36–40; Diod. XV. 92–3.
[3] Cf. p. 62.   [4] Plut. *Ages.* 4.   [5] XV. 19.

Agesilaus.[1] Agesipolis was succeeded by his younger brother Cleombrotus, who was hostile to Agesilaus, but too young, inexperienced and incompetent to cause much trouble. He too died after only nine years, leaving two infant sons, Agesipolis II, who died in a year, and Cleomenes II, of whom not a single action is recorded in his long and inglorious reign (370–309).

The main cause of Agesilaus' popularity was that his policy satisfied public opinion. There was some opposition to his more unscrupulous acts, such as the support he gave to Phoebidas and Sphodrias, but by and large the Spartans enjoyed wielding the big stick against their allies. The attack on Thebes which ended at Leuctra was voted enthusiastically by the Spartan assembly. Agesilaus cannot be held wholly responsible for the faults of Spartan policy, though he did much to exaggerate them.

After this Sparta almost fades from history for a century. This is partly because we no longer have a historian like Xenophon, interested in Spartan history, and partly because Sparta was now a second-rate power. Her domestic manpower was not, it is true, very greatly reduced, but she no longer had her submissive allies, on whom she had drawn so heavily. She now made even greater use of mercenaries. The kings and the ruling oligarchy were very rich and could afford to hire them on a large scale. They were, moreover, many of them military adventurers of the type that attracted mercenaries to their standard. Agesilaus was the first Spartan king to serve as a condottiere abroad. He was followed by his son Archidamus,[2] and later by Acrotatus,[3] Cleonymus[4] and his son Leonidas.[5] Later still it was the Spartiate Xanthippus who was appointed their commander in chief by the Carthaginians at a critical stage of the First Punic War.[6] By such adventures they acquired not only military prestige but wealth, with which to pay mercenaries in Spartan service.

It is significant that from the last quarter of the fourth century Taenarum became a great mercenary market. This could not

[1] Xen. *Hell.* V. iii. 20.   [2] Diod. XVI. 62–3.   [3] Diod. XIX. 70–1.
[4] Diod. XX. 104.   [5] Plut. *Agis*, 3.   [6] Polyb. I. 32.

have happened without the co-operation of the Spartan government, and suggests that it found it convenient to have a pool of mercenaries handy to draw upon, and also that mercenaries found the place convenient, perhaps because it was easy to get employment locally. The first suggestion that the market of Taenarum existed is in 333 B.C., when King Agis, shortly after the battle of Issus, received ships and money from the Persians and sent them to Taenarum.[1] It is not stated that his object was to hire mercenaries there, but it seems not unlikely. Taenarum next appears as a well known mercenary market, the best in Greece. Shortly before Alexander's death the mercenaries that he had discharged flocked, we are told, to Taenarum.[2] There were next year 8,000 available there to be hired for the Lamian War, and later in the year Thibron, a Spartan *condottiere* in Cyrenaica, enrolled 2,500 men for service there.[3] Eight years later Antigonus' agent Aristodemus raised 8,000 mercenaries with the consent of the Spartan government,[4] and in 303 Cleonymus raised 5,000 men at Taenarum for his western venture.[5]

Agesilaus' son Archidamus played a minor part in the Sacred War (356–346). When originally approached by the Phocian leader Philomelus he was friendly and gave him 15 talents,[6] and he later promised and sent help.[7] His motive was partly vengeance against Thebes, and partly the hope of obtaining Phocian aid against local enemies. Towards the end of the war Sparta did obtain 3,000 Phocians to assist her against Megalopolis, Argos, Messene and Sicyon—but to balance them 4,500 Thebans supported her enemies.[8] Archidamus then answered an appeal from the Lacedaemonian colony, Taras, to assist her against her barbarian neighbours. He died in Italy in 338.[9]

As the ally of Phocis in the Sacred War, Sparta naturally became the enemy of Philip of Macedon, and he naturally befriended her

[1] Arrian, *Anab.* II. 13. 6.   [2] Diod. XVII. 111.   [3] Diod. XVIII. 9, 21.
[4] Diod. XIX. 60   [5] Diod. XX. 104.   [6] Diod. XVI. 24.
[7] Diod. XVI. 27, 29, 37, 59.   [8] Diod. XVI. 39.
[9] Diod. XVI. 62–3; cf. Plut. *Agis*, 3; Paus. III. x. 5; Strabo, VI. 280.

enemies. After Chaeronea the Messenians, Argives and Megalo-politans invited Philip to the Peloponnese and he invaded Laconia, and, through the League of Corinth, adjudicated boundary disputes between these cities and Sparta in their favour.[1] Sparta refused to join the League of Corinth, alone of all the Greek cities.[2]

When Alexander disappeared into Asia in 331, King Agis of Sparta thought that his opportunity had come. He obtained 30 talents and 20 triremes from the Persians, and hired 8,000 mercenaries who had escaped from the battle of Issus.[3] Then when Memnon, Antipater's governor of Thrace, rebelled, he struck. He gained the alliance of Elis, Achaea and all the Arcadians except Megalopolis, raising an army of 32,000 men including 10,000 mercenaries. But he was still besieging Megalopolis when Antipater marched south and defeated and killed him.[4] The Spartans sent envoys of peace to Antipater, who referred them to the Corinthian League, which in turn remitted the question to Alexander.[5]

In the troubled years that followed Alexander's death, faced by the threat of Cassander's invasion of Greece (318), 'the terrified Spartans, contrary to the responses of the oracles and the ancient glory of their ancestors, distrusting their arms surrounded with the protection of walls the city which they had always defended with arms, not walls'.[6] Demetrius Poliorcetes defeated King Archidamus in 294, and would have captured Sparta but that he was diverted by attacks from Ptolemy and Lysimachus.[7] In the next generation Areus essayed a more ambitious foreign policy. Taking advantage of the weakening of Macedonia by the Gallic invasion of 280 he put himself at the head of all the Peloponnesian states, we are told, to fight the Aetolians. The alliance, however, soon broke up, as the other cities disliked Areus' autocratic

---

[1] Polyb. IX. 28, 33, XVIII. 14; cf. Tac. Ann. IV. 43; Paus. II. xx. 1; Strabo, VIII. 361.
[2] Justin, IX. v. 3; cf. Arrian, I. 17.   [3] Arrian II. 13; Diod. XVII. 48.
[4] Diod. XVII. 62–3; Deinarchus, I. 35; Aeschines, III. 165.
[5] Diod. XVII. 73.   [6] Justin, XIV. v. 6.   [7] Plut. Demetrius, 35.

methods.[1] Next, in 273 Pyrrhus, king of Epirus, took up the cause of Cleonymus, Areus' uncle.[2] His elder brother Acrotatus, who was unpopular at home, had left Sparta in 314 to take service under the Sicilian city of Acragas, but had later returned.[3] Then in 303 Taras had once again appealed for aid against the Lucanians, and Cleonymus, resentful that he had been passed over in favour of Acrotatus' son Areus, accepted the invitation, and raising 5,000 mercenaries sailed off to Italy. Here he soon quarrelled with his hosts, seized Corcyra and thus made contact with Pyrrhus, who took him into his service.[4]

Pyrrhus marched on Sparta with 25,000 infantry, 2,000 cavalry and 24 elephants. Areus was at the time away fighting in Crete, but his son Acrotatus managed to hold the city until his father returned with 2,000 mercenaries. Pyrrhus abandoned the siege, and Sparta still remained an uncaptured city.[5] Areus' prestige appears to have been enhanced by this success, and he built up an alliance comprising Elis, Achaea, Tegea, Mantinea, Orchomenus, Phigaleia, Caphyae (Sparta's old enemies Megalopolis, Argos and Messene remained recalcitrant), as well as a number of Cretan cities. In 266 he formed an alliance with Athens and with Ptolemy II of Egypt to fight Antigonus of Macedon. He advanced to the Isthmus, but the Ptolemaic fleet gave him no effective support, and he had to fall back on Corinth, where he was defeated and killed in 264.[6]

Sparta seems to have been exhausted by this effort, for some five years later Aristodemus, the tyrant of Megalopolis, defeated and killed Acrotatus, Areus' son and successor.[y] Some eight years later (251) we find Agis, son of Eudamidas, of the other royal family, fighting an alliance of Megalopolis and Mantinea, assisted by a force of Achaeans and Sicyonians under Aratus.[7] [z]

[1] Justin, XXIV. i. 1–7.   [2] Plut. *Pyrrhus*, 26.   [3] Diod. XIX. 70–1.
[4] Diod. XX. 104–5.   [5] Plut. *Pyrrhus*, 26 ff.
[6] *Syll.*[3] 434–5; Paus. I. i. 1, vii. 3, III. vi. 4–5; Justin XXVI. ii. 1; Plut. *Agis*, 3.
[7] Paus. VIII. xxvii. 9, VIII. x. 5–8.

XXV

AGIS AND CLEOMENES

IN 244 Agis IV came to the throne as a young man. His colleague was Leonidas, son of Cleonymus, who like his father had spent most of his active life soldiering abroad, but not in the west, but in the service of King Seleucus.[1] Spartans at this time had a high reputation as military experts and mercenary captains; we have seen how Acrotatus campaigned in Sicily, Cleonymus in Italy, Leonidas in the East, and even further afield Xanthippus reorganized the Carthaginian forces against Rome. But Sparta herself was lamentably weak, depending almost entirely on mercenaries for her wars.

Young Agis took the military weakness of this country much to heart, and brooded on its past glories, when the Lycurgan regime still flourished and the city could put thousands of well trained citizen hoplites into the field. By now the landed wealth of Laconia had passed into the hands of a narrow clique of wealthy families, and the Spartiates numbered scarcely 700, and most of them were poor men, heavily in debt.[2] Agis saw that the solution was a return to the Lycurgan regime, and in particular a redistribution of land such as Lycurgus was believed to have carried out.

Agis canvassed his ideas among the ruling oligarchy, and won over to his ideas several influential Spartiates.[3] Having secured the election of one of these, Lysander, to the ephorate, he got him to propose a *rhetra* in the *gerusia* for the abolition of debt and the redistribution of the land. Lysander duly introduced the measure into the *gerusia* and then put it before the assembly. He

---

[1] Plut. *Agis*, 3.   [2] Plut. *Agis*, 5.   [3] Plut. *Agis*, 6.

and two other of Agis' supporters, Agesilaus his uncle, and a certain Mandrocleidas, supported the motion, and Agis himself publicly surrendered his personal fortune, and that of his mother and grandmother. There were, he announced, to be 4,500 Spartiate lots, for which Perioeci would be eligible, and 15,000 perioecic lots.[1] The *pheiditia* were also to be revived, but in a new form: there were to be fifteen only[2] of them, with membership of 400 or 200, no longer intimate dining clubs but huge refectories. The only opposition came from the other king, Leonidas, who protested that abolition of debt and redistribution of land were unLycurgan novelties. The assembly was enthusiastic for the law, but the *gerusia* voted by a majority of one against it, and according to the ancient rule of the *rhetra* quashed the measure.[3]

Lysander responded by reviving another archaic rule. He watched the stars, and pronounced that Leonidas was not a lawful king, since he had married an Asiatic wife. Leonidas was deposed and took refuge in the temple of Athena Chalcioecus, but meanwhile a new board of ephors was elected who were hostile to the reform. They prosecuted Lysander and his colleague Mandrocleidas for illegal proceedings, but Agis claimed that the ephors had no right to resist the two kings if unanimous, and with the support of Cleombrotus, Leonidas' son, had a new board elected, including his uncle Agesilaus.[4]

Agesilaus was a wealthy landowner, but his estates were mortgaged. He pushed through the cancellation of debts, but delayed over the redistribution of land. Meanwhile the Achaean league demanded military aid from Sparta, and Agis marched out with his citizen army, and duly supported Aratus at Corinth. On his return he found that Agesilaus had alienated his supporters and was trying to make himself ephor for the second time. Leonidas was restored to the throne by the opposition and Agis and his colleague had to take sanctuary. Cleombrotus was exiled, and Agis was lured out of sanctuary, arrested by one of the ephors,

[1] Plut. *Agis*, 8–9.   [2] Plut. *Agis*, 8.   [3] Plut. *Agis*, 10, 11.   [4] Plut. *Agis*, 11, 12.

summarily tried before the *gerusia* and ephors, and put to death (241-0).[1]

Leonidas was succeeded in 237 by his son Cleomenes III. He, too, was zealous for Sparta's military revival, inspired by his wife Agiatis, Agis' widow, whom Leonidas had married to him because she was a very wealthy heiress.[2] But he bided his time, wishing to build up a military reputation. At this time Aratus the Achaean was trying to bring Sparta and Elis into the Achaean league, and was stirring up Megalopolis to aggression. Cleomenes, duly instructed by the ephors, seized the fortress of Athenaeum on the Megalopolitan border. Aratus captured Caphyae and Cleomenes, again on the ephors' orders, invaded the Argolid, and inflicted a defeat on Aratus and captured Mantinea and again defeated Aratus at Leuctra (227).[3]

Then he returned to Sparta, taking with him only his mercenaries, and staged an almost bloodless revolution. Four ephors were assassinated as they sat at dinner, and ten other Spartiates who supported them. Eighty others were exiled. Cleomenes then held an assembly, declared that the ephors had usurped excessive powers, contrary to the original constitution, and proclaimed the redistribution of the land. This time there were to be 4,000 citizens' lots, for which deserving Perioeci would be eligible; 80 lots were reserved for the exiles. Cleomenes abolished the ephorate, and also 'destroyed the power of the *gerusia*, instituting the *patronomi* nominally in their place'.[4] He revived the double kingship by appointing his brother Euclidas king; Archidamus, Agis' brother, had been recalled earlier in Cleomenes' reign, but had been murdered.[5]

Cleomenes was now in a position to establish Sparta's military supremacy in the Peloponnese. The Mantineans received him into their city, and he took Tegea; then he marched into Achaea and defeated the federal army under Aratus. Cleomenes now demanded that he should be made permanent commander in chief

<hr>

[1] Plut. *Agis*, 13–19.   [2] Plut. *Cleom.* 1.   [3] Plut. *Cleom.* 3–6.
[4] Paus. II. ix. 1.   [5] Plut. *Cleom.* 7–11, cf. 5.

of the league, and the Achaean assembly was prepared to agree, but Cleomenes failed to attend at the vital session. Aratus had no mind to abdicate his leadership of the Achaean league, and the war continued. The Achaeans called a second congress at Argos, but refused to allow Cleomenes to attend. Cleomenes promptly captured Pellene and then Argos, Cleonae and Phlius. His success was not purely military. The story of the Spartan revolution at home was known to everyone, and in every city the landless and indebted poor clamoured for abolition of debts and redistribution of land, and welcomed Cleomenes as their champion.[1]

Aratus now played his last card. He had won independence for the Achaean league by expelling the Macedonian garrison from Corinth. He now through the Megalopolitans, who had longstanding connections with Macedon, invited Antigonus to assist the league against Sparta, offering him the restitution of Corinth. Antigonus responded to his appeal and marched south. The tide now turned. The Argives, disappointed that no debts had been cancelled or land redistributed by Cleomenes, went over to Aratus. Cleomenes had to retreat to Sparta.[2] Here he raised money and men by selling their freedom to the Helots for 500 drachmas a head. He thus raised 50 talents to hire mercenaries and enrolled 2,000 Helots in his forces.[3]

The final battle took place at Sellasia in 222.[aa] Hopelessly outnumbered the Spartans were utterly defeated, and 6,000 of them killed. Cleomenes fled to Sparta and thence took ship to Alexandria.[4]

Agis and Cleomenes have been dubbed socialists. Their principal measures, abolition of debt and redistribution of land, did, it is true, correspond to the slogans of the extreme left throughout the Greek world. But they were not primarily moved by ideas of social justice, and they were certainly not egalitarians. Although they enrolled many new citizens they maintained the traditional

[1] Plut. *Cleom.* 12–16; Polyb. II. 45–6. [2] Plut. *Cleom.* 16–26; Polyb. II. 47–55.
[3] Plut. *Cleom.* 23. [4] Plut. *Cleom.* 27 ff.; Polyb. II. 65–9.

distinction of Spartiates, Perioeci and Helots. The last class in particular was vital to their whole policy, and Agis freed none, and Cleomenes only in the last crisis in order to raise money and increase his man power. It has also been claimed that they were inspired by Stoic ideas. It is true that a distinguished Stoic philosopher, Sphaerus of Borysthenes, strongly influenced Cleomenes when he was an adolescent in the reign of Agis; Sphaerus was at that time staying in Sparta and engaged in teaching the ephebes and young men.[1] But there is no indication that he inspired Agis' revolution, and chronological evidence that he can hardly have arrived in Sparta early enough to do so. Both kings were primarily Spartan patriots: it was their objective to restore Sparta as a powerful military state. Their policy was— or so they believed—traditional, to revive the original Lycurgan institutions. So naturally the revolution was domestic only, and was not promoted or encouraged in other cities.

[1] Plut. *Cleom.* 2.

XXVI

NABIS

A NTIGONUS restored the 'ancestral constitution' of Sparta, that is, the ephorate was restored, while the kingship remained in abeyance, Cleomenes being in exile. It is fairly certain that the redistribution of land was cancelled; the allottees had nearly all been killed at Sellasia. Sparta was thus left politically and militarily impotent.[1]

Two years later some ephebes attending a sacrifice by the ephors fell upon them and killed them, and also their supporters in the *gerusia*. New ephors were elected, and a demand was raised for the revival of the kingship, Cleomenes having been killed at Alexandria. From the Agiad royal house Agesipolis, son of Agesipolis, son of Cleombrotus, son of Leonidas, the legal heir, was chosen. From the other house, although there were several claimants in the direct line, Hippomedon, son of Agesilaus, son of Eudamidas and the sons of Archidamus, a certain Lycurgus was chosen 'who gave each of the ephors a talent to become a descendant of Heracles and king of Sparta';[2] he was probably a descendant of Agesilaus' illegitimate nephew, the son of Agis. The revolution meant a change of foreign policy. The previous government had been pro-Macedonian and pro-Achaean; the new was pro-Aetolian and launched a war against the Achaeans and Argives and Eleans.[3]

Two years later, Chilon, a rival claimant of Lycurgus to the throne, assassinated the ephors at dinner, and chased Lycurgus out of Sparta. His programme was a redistribution of land and he received much popular support at first, but he was overpowered

[1] Plut. *Cleom.* 30.   [2] Polyb. IV. 35.   [3] Polyb. IV. 36.

157

by his adversaries and fled.[1] Lycurgus returned and campaigned against Messene and Tegea.[2] This provoked an invasion of Laconia by Philip V, king of Macedon.[3] Soon after Lycurgus was suspected of revolutionary designs by the ephors and expelled.[4] He was recalled a year later and invaded Messenia (217).[5]

Lycurgus at some time expelled his colleague Agesipolis and reigned alone.[6] He was succeeded by his infant son, Pelops, for whom Machanidas was regent. Machanidas was no doubt a member of the royal family, but his relationship to Pelops is unknown. Machanidas became an ally of Rome in the First Macedonian War[7] and was decisively defeated and killed at Mantinea in 206 by the Achaeans under Philopoemen.[8] He was succeeded as regent by Nabis[9] who later made away with Pelops. Nabis is always styled a tyrant by Polybius and Livy, but he called himself King, and was apparently a genuine Eurypontid, descended from King Demaratus, who had been deposed by Cleomenes I and taken refuge in Persian territory. His descendants can be traced ruling a little principality in the Troad in the fourth century[10] and intermarrying with another Greek dynasty, descended from the traitor Gongylos. Under Lysimachus Demaratus son of Gorgion, a Spartan, was honoured by the Delians,[11] and Nabis himself was son of Demaratus.[12]

Nabis was a thorough-going revolutionary. He exiled the wealthy and the nobles, and distributed their estates to the local population and to his mercenaries: he made it unsafe for the exiles to live anywhere near Sparta by hiring assassins to waylay them.[13] He freed and enfranchised many slaves, but not apparently the Helots, who were the necessary base of the Lycurgan system.[14] Abroad he pursued the usual anti-Achaean and anti-Macedonian policy of Sparta, allying himself with the Aetolians, Elis and

[1] Polyb. IV. 81.   [2] Polyb. V. 17.   [3] Polyb. V. 18–24.
[4] Polyb. V. 29.   [5] Polyb. V. 91–2.   [6] Livy, XXXIV. 26.
[7] Livy, XXVII. 29, XXVIII. 5, 7.   [8] Polyb. XI. 11–18.
[9] Polyb. XIII. 6; Diod. XXVII. 1; cf. Livy, XXXIV. 32.
[10] Xen. *Hell.* III. i. 6; *Anab.* II. i. 3, VII. viii. 17.   [11] *Syll.*[3] 381.
[12] *Syll*[3]. 584.   [13] Polyb. XIII. 6–8.   [14] Livy, XXXIV. 27.

Messene.[1] As such he too became an ally of Rome in the First Macedonian War.[2]

When the Achaeans deserted Philip and allied themselves with Rome, and Flamininus advanced into Euboea, Philip, wishing to concentrate his forces, surrendered Argos to Nabis on the understanding that he would restore it to him if he won the war. Here, too, Nabis carried through a social revolution, abolishing debts and redistributing the land.[3] In 195, when the war was over and the Greeks had been liberated, the senate decided that, in view of the probable advance of Antiochus into Greece, Nabis must be dealt with, and Flamininus was empowered to take what action he thought proper.[4] He summoned a congress of all the allied cities at Corinth, and put it to them whether they would tolerate Argos being occupied by the tyrant. All agreed that action must be taken; and the allied forces marched to Argos.[5] The governor, Pythagoras, brother of Nabis' wife and his son-in-law, suppressed a local rising, led by a young noble, Damocles, and Flamininus, finding the resistance firm, decided to divert his attack to Sparta itself.[6] Pythagoras evacuated Argos, and marched to Sparta with 1,000 mercenaries and 2,000 Argives, leaving Timocrates of Pella in charge of the city.[7] Nabis had 2,000 Cretans, 3,000 mercenaries, 10,000 Lacedaemonians and a Helot levy. Against him were mustered 50,000 troops.[8]

Nabis took no risks of treachery. He arrested and executed 80 young men whose loyalty was suspect, and had a number of Helots who had tried to desert flogged through the streets.[9] Flamininus' first move was to occupy the coastal Perioecic cities. No resistance was met except at Gytheum and even here the two commanders soon surrendered the town on condition of being allowed to march the garrison to Sparta.[10]

Nabis now asked for a parley. He claimed that he was an ally of the Roman people, and had never broken his treaty of alliance.

[1] Polyb. XVI. 13. [2] Livy, XXIX. 12, XXXIV. 31.
[3] Livy, XXXII. 38. [4] Livy, XXXIII. 44–5. [5] Livy, XXXIV. 22–4.
[6] Livy, XXXIV. 25–6. [7] Livy, XXXIV. 29. [8] Livy, XXXIV. 27, 38.
[9] Livy, XXXIV. 27. [10] Livy, XXXIV. 29.

If he was charged with freeing slaves and distributing the land to the poor, he was acting according to the ancestral tradition of Sparta. The Romans might select their cavalry and infantry according to property qualifications. 'Our lawgiver did not want the state to be in the hands of the few, what you call the senate, nor that one or another class should have supremacy in the state; but he believed that by equality of fortune and dignity there would be many to bear arms for their country.'[1]

Flamininus replied that Sparta must be restored to its ancient freedom and to its own laws, to which Nabis had just alluded as if he was a disciple of Lycurgus.[2] Next day Nabis offered to surrender Argos and restore prisoners and deserters. A council was held in which the majority declared for war to finish with the tyrant, but Flamininus advised coming to terms.[3]

The terms he proposed were a six months truce during which envoys should be sent to Rome by Flamininus and Nabis to ratify the proposed treaty. Nabis must surrender Argos in ten days. He must restore to the maritime cities the ships that he had taken from them, and himself maintain no more than two *lembi* of sixteen rowers. He must restore all prisoners and deserters to their cities, and their wives and children (if they so wished) to the Spartan exiles. He was to hold no city in Crete, nor form any alliance with a Cretan city for the future. He was to give five hostages, including his son, and 100 talents forthwith, and 50 per annum for eight years.[4]

Nabis himself did not find these terms intolerable. It was a great thing that he would not have to receive back the exiles. His greatest loss would be the Perioecic towns, which provided a large part of his army and all his fleet.[5] He held an assembly which unanimously voted to carry on the war.[6] Flamininus pressed the siege for three days and Nabis then accepted the terms offered. At this moment news came that Argos had expelled its garrison.[7]

[1] Livy, XXXIV. 30–1.   [2] Livy, XXXIV. 32.   [3] Livy, XXXIV. 33–4.
[4] Livy, XXXIV. 35.   [5] Livy, XXXIV. 36.   [6] Livy, XXXIV. 37.
[7] Livy, XXXIV. 38–40.

When Antiochus was expected to invade Greece, Nabis, encouraged by the Aetolians, reoccupied the coastal cities. The charge of protecting these coastal cities had been entrusted by Flamininus to the Achaeans and they sent troops to Gytheum and envoys to Rome.[1] While Nabis promptly pressed the attack on Gytheum, the Achaeans awaited the return of the envoys from Rome. They brought instructions to await the arrival of a Roman fleet, but the Achaean assembly, spurred on by Philopoemen, decided to reject this advice.[2] Nabis had only three warships and a few *lembi*, but the Achaean fleet was even feebler, its flagship being a rotten old quadrireme captured 40 years before, and was promptly routed.[3] Nabis stormed Gytheum, but Philopoemen eventually shut him up in Sparta and, having ravaged Laconian territory for a month, marched home.[4] A few months later the Aetolians sent a force of 1,000 infantry to Sparta to support Nabis should he declare for Antiochus. Their leader Alexamenus treacherously murdered the king on parade (192). Next day the Spartans rose, proclaimed Laconicus, a member of the royal family, but not a son of Nabis, king (he is never heard of again), and slaughtered the Aetolians.[5] Philopoemen on hearing of the death of Nabis, went to Sparta and assisted by the arrival of a Roman fleet at Gytheum, enrolled the city in the Achaean league.[6] So died the last great king of Sparta, a worthy successor of Cleomenes III, and a true disciple of the mythical Lycurgus. Nabis too was no socialist, but a Spartan patriot. He enrolled thousands of new citizens from his mercenaries, but like Agis and Cleomenes he preserved the hierarchy of Spartiates, Perioeci and Helots. More realistic than they, however, he saw the propaganda value of the revolutionary programme and extended it to other cities which he acquired.

Philopoemen won great glory by incorporating Sparta in the Achaean league, but he was not satisfied. As an aristocrat he loathed the democratic regime of Sparta, and had strong sympathy

[1] Livy, XXXV. 12–13.   [2] Livy, XXXV. 25.   [3] Livy, XXXIV. 26.
[4] Livy, XXXIV. 27–30.   [5] Livy, XXXV. 35–6.   [6] Livy, XXXV. 37.

with the exiles still excluded from the city. As a Megalopolitan he was obsessed by a fear of Sparta, and determined to render her impotent. When in 190 the Spartans sent an embassy to ask for the return of their hostages, and for 'the villages' (presumably the Perioecic towns), the senate expressed its surprise that the Spartans, now that they were freed, did not receive back the 'old exiles' (one may guess who inspired this advice), but allowed the return of the hostages except for Nabis' son Armenas. The question of the villages it referred to the Roman envoys on the spot, and they apparently gave no satisfaction.[1]

Next year the Spartans, finding it intolerable to have no port through which they could receive imports from abroad or despatch their envoys abroad—the exiles were dominant in the Perioecic cities—seized Las. They were forthwith expelled, but Philopoemen now had his opportunity. Summoning an assembly of the Achaean league he solemnly declared that by the seizure of Las, which the Romans had placed under Achaean protection, Sparta had broken the treaty, and must surrender those responsible to the Achaeans. The Spartans were naturally indignant at this curt order, and fearful that it was the thin end of the wedge, a prelude to the return of the exiles, they executed 30 members of the pro-Achaean faction, denounced their membership of the Achaean league, and sent envoys to the Roman consul Fulvius, who was in Cephallenia, offering to surrender Sparta to Rome.[2]

The Achaean assembly declared war, but as it was winter no immediate military action was taken. The consul Fulvius summoned the Spartans and the Achaeans to Elis, and when they failed to agree, ordered both parties to keep the peace and send embassies to Rome: the Spartan exiles accompanied the Achaean envoys. One of the Achaean envoys, Diophanes, left the whole matter to the senate. The other, Lycortas, urged that the Achaean league, being free and independent, should be allowed to settle its own affairs. The senate returned an ambiguous answer, and

[1] Polyb. XXI. 1, 3.   [2] Livy, XXXVIII. 30–1.

162

Philopoemen, re-elected general, marched on Sparta, and demanded the surrender of those responsible for the revolt, promising that they should have fair trial. When the Spartans approached the Achaean camp they were insulted and assaulted by the exiles, and seventeen were lynched. Next day 63 were summarily condemned to death and executed (188).[1]

The terms imposed were that all Nabis' former mercenaries and all the slaves whom he had freed should leave Laconia. Any who remained would be sold as slaves by the Achaeans. The walls were to be demolished. The district of Belbine was to be surrendered to Megalopolis. The Lycurgan constitution was to be abolished and Achaean laws and institutions introduced; even the training of the ephebes was to be on the Achaean model. Two inscribed decrees,[2] in themselves of trivial content (grants of *proxenia*), show how thoroughgoing Philopoemen was. The movers of the decrees approach the boards of magistrates in Achaean fashion, the decrees are passed by the people without reference to the ephors, and the money is supplied by the *epidamiurgus*—*damiurgos* was the standard title of Achaean magistrates. Three thousand of the former mercenaries and slaves, who went into hiding in the countryside, were hunted down and sold, and from the profits a portico was built at Megalopolis.[3]

The returned exiles were as proud of Sparta's Lycurgan institutions and as resentful of foreign control as Nabis and his people had been, and were not grateful to Philopoemen. The Lycurgan constitution was soon restored,[4] and in 185 two of the aristocratic leaders, Areus and Alcibiades, went to Rome to complain of the highhanded proceedings of the Achaeans. The consul Lepidus wrote rebuking the Achaeans, who sent a counter embassy, and the matter was referred to Caecilius Metellus, then in Greece on a mission to Philip. He asked for an assembly of the Achaean league, but was refused, on the ground that he had no

[1] Livy, XXXVIII. 32–3.
[3] Livy, XXXVIII. 34; Plut. *Philopoemen*, 16.
[2] IG V. i. 4–5.
[4] Plut. *Philopoemen*, 16.

letter from the senate to present to the Achaeans.[1] Next year another Roman envoy, Appius Claudius, dealt with the issue. He asked that the condemnation of Areus and Alcibiades should be cancelled, and that in future Spartans must be tried for federal offences not by the Achaean assembly, but by a third state. He allowed Sparta to rebuild her walls, but he did not allow her to secede from the Achaean league.[2]

She did so none the less a few years later and in 180 resumed her membership; the intransigent 'old exiles' had by now fallen from power.[3]

In 154, a Rome commissioner, Gallus, adjudicated a boundary dispute between Sparta and Argos. A few years later the Achaean league condemned a Spartan, Menalcidas, to death, for having served as envoy to Rome contrary to Achaean interests, and advocating the secession of Sparta from the league. War broke out, and the matter was referred to the senate. In 146 Metellus, in command of a Roman army sent to reduce the Macedonian pretender Andriscus, tried to stop the war. This war was one of the principal reasons why the Roman consul Mummius fought and crushed the Achaean league, and made Greece a Roman province.[4]

Sparta was, naturally, not included in the province, remaining a free city.[5]

[1] Polyb. XXII. 1, 10–12; Paus. VII. viii. 6, ix. 1.
[2] Livy, XXXIX. 35–7, 48; Paus. VII. ix. 3 ff.   [3] Polyb. XXIII. 17.
[4] Paus. VII. xi ff.   [5] Pliny, NH IV. 16; Strabo, VIII, 365.

XXVII

SPARTA UNDER ROMAN RULE

THE history of Sparta is thereafter a blank for more than a century. Antony executed a prominent Spartan noble, Lachares, who had probably received the Roman citizenship from Julius Caesar, for piracy. As a result a Spartan squadron, led by Lachares' son, Eurycles, fought for Caesar's heir against Antony at Actium,[1] and when Caesar's heir won the day, Sparta received her reward. The freedom of twenty-four formerly Perioecic cities, the Eleutherolacones, was confirmed, but several former Perioecic cities were subjected to Sparta. These included the island of Cythera and Thuria, Pharae, and Cardamyle at the head of the Messenian gulf: Sparta thus had access to the sea.[2] C. Julius Eurycles, relying on his great wealth—he owned Cythera —and his personal friendship with Augustus, seems to have established a dominance, almost amounting to autocracy, in Sparta, but later in Augustus' reign he fell from favour. His son C. Julius Laco later succeeded to his power.[3]

From this period Spartan inscriptions begin to be abundant, and it is possible to reconstruct the constitution and the social life of the city. The Lycurgan constitution was not fully restored. There were inevitably no kings, both royal lines having died out, and the place of the kings was taken by a annual board of six *patronomi*, whose chief gave his name to the year.[4] The *gerousia*, which in the absence of the kings still numbered 28, had become an annually elected body, and it would appear that the five ephors

[1] Plut. *Ant.* 67.
[2] Strabo, VIII. 363, Paus. III. xxi. 6–7, xxvi. 7, IV. xxx. 2, xxxi. 1. 301, ff.
[3] Strabo, VIII. 363, 366, cf. coins with his name, and Josephus, *Ant. Jud.* XVI. 301 ff. *Bell. Jud.* I. 513 ff.; Tac. *Ann.* VI. 18. Cf. *JRS* LI (1961), pp. 112–18.
[4] *IG.* V. i. 48–77.

were *ex officio* members, leaving 23 ordinary seats.[1] The ephors still existed[2] and the *paedonomus*, who supervised the training of the boys and ephebes, but there were now also six *gynaeconomi*,[3] an unLycurgan innovation, who controlled the behaviour of the women. Other magistrates included the five *bideoi*,[4] the meaning of whose archaic title is uncertain, the *agoranomi*,[5] and the *nomophylaces* or guardians of the laws.[6] To advise them there were 'instructors in Lycurgan customs' and 'expositors of Lycurgan customs'.[7]

The training of the boys and youths was strictly maintained. The latter were organized in year-groups or 'herds', each under a senior youth, the 'herdsman', and known by strange archaic names.[8] For adults the dining clubs of *pheiditia* still subsisted.[9]

The structure of Spartan society seems to have been highly aristocratic and only a small group of noble families were eligible for the office of *patronomus*. Other offices were, however, open to a wider group, who had completed the discipline. This was open not only to the sons of nobles, but to commoners who were adopted by them.[10]

The ancient festivals of Sparta, the Gymnopaedia and the Carneia, were celebrated with splendour, and the boxing matches between the boys of the obes (now raised to six by the addition of the Neopolitae), continued. The boys still snatched cheeses from the altar of Artemis Orthia, and a little theatre was built for their elders and numerous tourists to watch the brutal game. Libanius, visiting Sparta in the reign of Constantius II, saw the 'Laconian festival, the Whips'.[11]

So ends the history of one of the most conservative communities of history.

---

[1] *IG.* V. i. 92–122.   [2] *IG.* V. i. 48–77.   [3] *IG.* V. i. 170.
[4] *IG.* V. i. 136–40; Paus. III. xi. 2, xii. 4.   [5] *IG.* V. i. 124–9.
[6] *IG.* V. i. 78–91; Paus. III. xi. 2.   [7] *IG.* V. i. 500, 554.
[8] *IG.* V. i. 273 ff.   [9] *IG.* V. i. 128, 150, 155, 1507.
[10] Chrimes, *Ancient Sparta*, 84 ff.   [11] Libanius, *Or.* I. 23.

SELECT BIBLIOGRAPHY

A. ANDREWES, 'Eunomia', *CQ* XXXII (1938), 89–102.

— 'Sparta and Arcadia in the Early Fifth Century', *Phoenix* VI (1952), 1–5.

— 'The Government of Classical Sparta', in *Studies of Ancient Politics and Society in Honour of Victor Ehrenberg*, 1966.

P. A. BRUNT, 'Spartan Policy and Strategy in the Archidamian War', *Phoenix* XIX (1965), 255–80.

G. BUSOLT, H. SWOBODA, *Griechische Staatskunde*,³ Münich, 1926.

D. BUTLER, 'Competence of the Demos in the Spartan Rhetra', *Historia* XI (1962), 385–96.

K. M. T. CHRIMES, *Ancient Sparta*, Manchester, 1949.

R. M. COOK, 'Spartan History and Archaeology', *CQ* XII (1962), 156–8.

W. DEN BOER, *Laconian Studies*, Amsterdam, 1954.

G. DICKENS, 'The growth of Spartan policy', *JHS* XXXII (1912), 1–26.

V. EHRENBERG, *Neugründer des Staates*, Münich, 1925.

— 'Der Gesetzgeber von Sparta', in *Epitymbion für Swobode*, 1927.

— 'Sparta (Geschichte)' in *PW*.

W. G. FORREST, 'The Date of the Lykourgan Reforms in Sparta', *Phoenix* XVII (1963), 157–79.

G. GILBERT, *The Constitutional Antiquities of Sparta and Athens*, London, 1895.

A. H. J. GREENIDGE, *Greek Constitutional History*, London, 1928.

G. B. GRUNDY, 'The Policy of Sparta', *JHS* XXXII (1912), 261–9.

N. G. L. HAMMOND, 'The Lycurgean Reform at Sparta', *JHS* LXX (1950), 42–64.

W. W. HOW and J. WELLS, 'Sparta under King Cleomenes', in *Commentary on Herodotus*, Oxford 1912.

G. L. HUXLEY, *Early Sparta*, London, 1962.

F. JACOBY, *Apollodors Chronik*, Berlin, 1902.

L. H. JEFFERY, 'Commentary on some Archaic Greek Inscriptions', *JHS* LXIX (1949), 25–38.

A. H. M. JONES, 'Two Synods of the Delian and the Peloponnesian Leagues', *Proc. Camb. Phil. Soc.* 1952–3, 43–6.

— 'The Lycurgan Rhetra', *Studies of Ancient Politics and Society in Honour of Victor Ehrenberg*, 1966.

J. A. O. LARSEN, 'The Constitution of the Peloponnesian League', *CP* XXVII (1932), 136–50; XXVIII (1933), 257–76; XXIX (1934), 1–19.

D. LOTZE, Μόθακες, *Historia* XI (1962), 427–35.

H. MICHELL, *Sparta*, Cambridge, 1952.

M. P. NILSSON, 'Die Gründlagen des Spartanischen Lebens', *Klio* XII (1912), 308–40.

F. OLLIER, *Xénophon, la république des Lacedémoniens*, Lyons, 1934.

— *Le Mirage Spartiate*, Vol. I, Paris, 1933; Vol. II, Paris, 1943.

H. W. PARKE, 'The Development of the Second Spartan Empire', *JHS* L (1930), 37–79.

— 'The Tithe of Apollo and the Harmost at Decelea, 413–404 B.C.', *JHS* LII (1932), 42–6.

L. PEARSON, 'The Pseudo-History of Messenia and its Authors', *Historia*, XI (1962), 397–426.

P. PORALLA, *Prosopographie der Lakedaemonier*, Breslau, 1913.

E. SMITH, 'The Opposition to Agesilaus' Foreign Policy, 394–71 B.C.', *Historia* II (1954), 274–87.

A. J. TOYNBEE, 'The Growth of Sparta', *JHS* XXXIII (1913), 246–75.

M. TREU, 'Der Schlusssatz der grossen Rhetra', *Hermes* LXXVI (1941), 22–42.

G. E. UNDERHILL, 'Sparta' (pp. 334–53), in *Commentary on the Hellenica of Xenophon*, Oxford, 1900.

A. VON BLUMENTHAAL, 'Zur "Lykurgischen" Rhetra', *Hermes* LXXVI (1942), 212–15.

H. T. WADE-GERY, 'The Spartan Rhetra in Plutarch', *Lycurgus* VI, CQ XXXVI (1943), 57–78; XXXVIII (1944), 1–9, 115–26, reprinted in *Essays in Greek History*, Oxford, 1958.

W. P. WALLACE, 'Kleomenes, Marathon, the Helots and Arkadia', *JHS* LXXIV (1954), 32–5.

M. E. WHITE, 'Some Agiad dates; Pausanias and his sons', *JHS* LXXIV (1964), 140–52.

ADDITIONAL NOTES

ᵃ Many attempts have been made, all equally unsuccessful, to reconcile the Eurypontid genealogies in Herodotus and Pausanias. The Oxford text shamelessly prints ἕπτα for δυό in Herod. VIII. 131. This is (a) palaeographically arbitrary; (b) in sense unnatural; one does not say all except seven of fifteen ancestors were kings of Sparta; (c) historically unlikely. It is remotely improbable that seven generations of Spartan kings had one surviving son and one only. The question has been last discussed by W. Den Boer (*Laconian Studies*, 65ff.), who cites the previous literature. His own solution is ingenious, that the Spartans told Herodotus all Leotychides' ancestors had been kings except for the last two γενεαί, meaning centuries. But it is still open to objection (c).

ᵇ The Spartan chronology of Apollodorus and Sosibius is analysed in Jacoby, *Apollodors Chronik*, pp. 75–91, 108–18, 122–42.

ᶜ Jeanmaire, (*REG* XXVI (1913), pp. 121 ff., 'La Cryptie Lacédémonienne') prefers to believe with Plato (*Laws*, VI, 760 ff. and the scholiast) that the Krypteia was a kind of boy scout training in tracking. I prefer to believe the factual Aristotle rather than the idealizing Plato.

ᵈ The original *gerousia* was presumably composed of nobles only. On the later *gerousia* the language of Aristotle is ambiguous. When he says that all elements at Sparta desire the preservation of the constitution, the kings for the sake of their own honour, οἱ δὲ καλοὶ κἀγαθοὶ διὰ τὴν γερουσίαν (ἆθλον γὰρ ἡ ἀρχὴ αὕτη τῆς ἀρετῆς ἐστιν), ὁ δὲ δῆμος διὰ τὴν ἐφορείαν· καθίσταται γὰρ ἐξ ἁπάντων (*Pol.* II. ix. 22, 1270b) he is probably using the terms καλοὶ κἀγαθοί and ἀρετή in a moral sense. Doubtless also he has in mind that the ordinary commoner had very little chance in practice of becoming an elder, whereas he might well be elected ephor. Similarly when he says (*Pol.* IV. ix. 9, 1294b) ἔτι τὸ δύο τὰς μεγίστας ἀρχὰς τὴν μὲν αἱρεῖσθαι τὸν δῆμον τῆς δὲ μετέχειν· τοὺς μὲν γὰρ γέροντας αἱροῦνται, τῆς δ' ἐφορείας μετέχουσι, he is probably thinking of the practical facts. Again, when he speaks of those who praise the Spartan constitution as mixed, the kingship representing monarchy, τὴν δὲ τῶν γερόντων ἀρχὴν ὀλιγαρχίαν, δημοκρατεῖσθαι δὲ κατὰ τὴν τῶν ἐφόρων ἀρχὴν διὰ τὸ ἐκ τοῦ δήμου εἶναι τοὺς ἐφόρους (*Pol.* II. vi. 17, 1265b), he does not necessarily imply that the elders were chosen from a limited group. A small council which sat for life was to his mind oligarchic however constituted, and in practice again few humble citizens would obtain a seat. The most difficult passage is *Pol.* V. vi.

11, 1306a, when he says that at Elis τῆς πολιτείας γὰρ δι' ὀλίγων οὔσης τῶν γερόντων ὀλίγοι πάμπαν ἐγίνοντο διὰ τὸ ἀιδίους εἶναι ἐνενήκοντα ὄντας, τὴν δ' αἵρεσιν δυναστευτικὴν εἶναι καὶ ὁμοίαν τῇ τῶν ἐν Λακεδαίμονι γερόντων. The words δυναστεία and δυναστευτικός seem basically to denote the irresponsible rule of a small group (bearing the same relationship to oligarchy as tyranny to kingship), e.g. Pol. V. vi. 12, 1306a, IV. xiv, 7, 1298a, but added to this there is sometimes the notion of a hereditary group where son succeeds father, as in IV. v. 2, 1292b, and IV. vi. 11, 1293a. It is difficult to see how the adjective could apply to the elections to the Spartan gerousia, where son certainly did not automatically succeed father. It is tempting to follow Sauppe and insert an οὐχ before ὁμοίαν. If the text is sound, Aristotle must be writing very loosely and meaning that the general character of the gerousia was δυναστευτική, that is, that it was a small group which exercised arbitrary authority without due control of law. He comments elsewhere (Pol. II. ix. 25–6, 1270b–71a) on the irresponsibility of its members. Polybius (VI. 10), describing the mixed constitution of Sparta, speaks of the elders, οἱ κατ' ἐκλογὴν ἀριστίνδην κεκριμένοι πάντες ἔμελλον ἀεὶ τῷ δικαίῳ προσνέμειν ἑαυτούς; he appears to be using ἀριστίνδην in a moral sense.

As against this dubious language must be set the testimony of Xenophon (Resp. Lac. x. 1–3), Demosthenes (XX. 107) and Plutarch (Lyc. 26), who regard election to the gerousia as a reward of merit, and say nothing about birth.

e The text of Plutarch's citation from Tyrtaeus is:

Φοίβου ἀκούσαντες Πυθωνόθεν οἴκαδ' ἔνεικαν
μαντείας τε θεοῦ καὶ τελέεντ' ἔπεα·
ἄρχειν μὲν βουλῆς θεοτιμήτους βασιλῆας,
οἷσι μέλει Σπάρτης ἱμερόεσσα πόλις,
πρεσβύτας τε γέροντας, ἔπειτα δὲ δημότας ἄνδρας
εὐθείαις ῥήτραις ἀνταπαμειβομένους.

Diodorus' version is:

ἡ Πυθία ἔχρησε τῷ Λυκούργῳ περὶ τῶν πολιτικῶν οὕτως
δὲ γὰρ ἀργυρότοξος ἄναξ ἑκάεργος Ἀπόλλων
χρυσοκόμης ἔχρη πίονος ἐξ ἀδύτου
ἄρχειν μὲν βουλῇ θεοτιμήτους βασιλῆας
οἷσι μέλει Σπάρτης ἵχερόεσσα πόλις
πρεσβυγενεῖς δὲ γέροντας ἔπειτα δὲ δημότας ἄνδρας
εὐθείην ῥήτρας ἀνταπαμειβομένους
μυθεῖσθαι δὲ τὰ καλὰ καὶ ἔρδειν πάντα δίκαια

171

μηδέτι ἐπιβουλεύειν τῇδε πόλει
δήμου τε πλήθει νίκην καὶ κάρτος ἕπεσθαι
Φοῖβος γὰρ περὶ τῶν ὧδ' ἀνέφηνε πόλει

This can be readily emended to make sense: ὧδε for δὲ in line 1, βουλῆς in line 3, εὐθείας in line 6, τε for δὲ in line 7, and μηδέ τι βουλεύειν τῇδε πόλει ⟨βλαβερόν⟩ in line 8. The style is a trifle prosaic, but so is much of Tyrtaeus. The chief objection to its authenticity would be that Plutarch does not quote it, though it is so apposite, but for the fact that it certainly was current by his day.

ᶠ The text of the *rhetra* in Plutarch runs:

Διὸς Συλλανίου καὶ 'Αθηνᾶς Συλλανίας ἱερὸν ἱδρυσάμενον (mss.-ος) φυλὰς φυλάξαντα καὶ ὠβὰς ὠβάξαντα τριάκοντα γερουσίαν σὺν ἀρχαγέταις καταστήσαντα ὥρας ἐξ ὥρας ἀπελλάζειν μεταξὺ Βαβύκας τε καὶ Κνακίωνος οὕτως εἰσφέρειν τε καὶ ἀφίστασθαι γαμωδᾶν γορίαν ἦ μὴν καὶ κράτος.

αἱ δὲ σκολιὰν ὁ δᾶμος ἕροιτο τοὺς πρεσβυγενέας καὶ ἀρχαγέτας ἀποστατῆρας εἶμεν.

It is discussed in H. T. Wade-Gery, *Essays in Greek History*, pp. 37 ff.; M. Treu, *Hermes* LXXVI (1941), pp. 22 ff.; A. Von Blumenthal, *Hermes* LXXVI (1942), pp. 212 ff.; N. G. L. Hammond, *JHS* LXX (1950), pp. 42 ff. I would prefer to read with Wade-Gery τούτως or αὐτώς (they) for οὕτως. For the corrupt passage various suggestions have been: (1) δάμῳ δὲ τὰν κυρίαν ἦμεν καὶ κράτος (Teubner); (2) δάμῳ δ'ἀνταγορίαν ἦμεν καί κράτος (Wade-Gery); (3) δαμωδᾶν γορίαν ἦμεν καὶ κράτος (Von Blumenthal). I prefer No. (2), translating ἀνταγορίαν as 'refusal'. I have dealt with the constitutional interpretation in *Studies of Ancient Politics and Society in Honour of Victor Ehrenberg*, where I deal briefly with rival views.

ᵍ This view of the ephorate is presented in an extreme form by G. Dickens, *JHS* XXXII (1912), 1-26, but underlies much speculation about Spartan politics, especially in the reign of Cleomenes.

ʰ On the obes see H. T. Wade-Gery, *Essays in Greek History*, pp. 74 ff.; I do not find Professor Beattie's new obe convincing (CQI (1951), pp. 46-8).

ⁱ The lines of Tyrtaeus *Anth. Lyr. Gr.*³ fr. 1 run:

[ἀλλ' ἴομε]ν κοίλησ' ἀσπίσι φραξάμ[ενοι]
χωρὶς Πάμφυλοί τε καὶ 'Υλλεῖς ἠδ[ὲ Δυμᾶνες]
ἀνδροφόνους μελίας χερσὶν ἀν[ασχόμενοι]
[   ]δ' ἀθανάτοισι θεοῖσ' ἐπὶ πάν[τα τιθέντες]
[ὄκνου] ἄτερ μονίηι πεισόμεθ᾽ ἡγεμ[όνων]

See Hammond's comments in *JHS* LXX (1950), pp. 50-1.

j Jacoby in *Apollodors Chronik*, p. 138–42, claims that the date for the foundation of the ephorate can have been derived only from a complete ephor list.

k This war is dated by Pausanias (III. vii. 3) to the reign of Charilaus, i.e. immediately after the Lycurgan reforms, as Herodotus (I. 65–6) says. I believe that it happened not long before the second and successful Tegeate war, as Herodotus implies.

l The rather confused passage from Diogenes Laertius is analysed by Jacoby, *Apollodors Chronik*, pp. 183–8. This date can with difficulty be reconciled with the story in Herod. I. 59, that Chilon was a grown man when Peisistratus was born.

m N. G. L. Hammond has tried to retrieve the veracity of *P.Ryl.* 18 in *CQ* VI (1956), pp. 49 ff. I find it difficult to believe that there was another tyrant called Hippias a generation earlier in another city, and still more that Herodotus omitted Sparta's alleged part in Pisistratus' second expulsion.

n Aeschines of Sicyon is only mentioned in *P.Ryl.* 18 and Plutarch *de Malignitate Herodoti*, who may well be dependent on *P.Ryl.* 18. He is conspicuously absent from the accounts of the tyranny in Herod. V. 67–8, VI. 126–30, Arist. *Pol.* V. xii, 1, 12, 1315b, 1316a, Nicolaus of Damascus (*FGH* 90, F61), Paus. II. viii. 1.

o Pausanias (III. vii. 5) records a war about Thyreatis in the last years of Theopompus. He also records an Argive victory over the Spartans in 669 at Hysiae (II. xxiv. 7); the story apparently comes from an Argive source and the date may be calculated according to a different scheme from those of the Spartan kings. Hysiae might therefore be the final battle of Theopompus' war or belong to a later war, but in either case Thyreatis would not have been permanently acquired by Sparta. Herodotus (I. 82) implies that the conquest took place just before the Battle of the Champions. Chilon's remark (Herod. VII. 235) that it would be better for the Spartans if Cythera were sunk under the sea suggests that it was in hostile hands in his day.

p There is an old and by now defunct crux about the date of the Plataean alliance; see A. W. Gomme, *Commentary on Thucydides*, II, p. 358.

q There is another old and by now almost defunct crux on the battle of Sepeia, because Pausanias (III, iv. 1. 1) says that it occurred at the beginning of Cleomenes' reign. The arguments are set out in W. W. How and J. Wells, *Commentary on Herodotus*, II, p. 352.

r The tissue of conjectures woven by Jacoby (*FGH* IIIa, pp. 117 ff.) to prove that Rhianus wrote about a Messenian war at the time of Marathon has been thoroughly swept up by L. Pearson in *Historia*, XI (1962), 418 ff. Nor do I find Miss L. H. Jeffery's arguments in *JHS* LXIX (1949), 25–38, very

173

convincing. The inscription is no doubt of early fifth century date, but there is nothing except guide's gossip (Paus. V. xxiv. 3) to connect it with a Messenian war. The same applies to the two bronze tripods by Gitiadas (Paus. III. xviii. 7–8, cf. IV. xiv. 2).

ˢ The well known crux on the dates of Themistocles' ostracism and flight to Persia (see A. W. Gomme, *Commentary on Thucydides* I. pp. 397–401) has been solved by M. E. White, *JHS* LXXXIV (1964), pp. 140 ff.

ᵗ I forbear to discuss the disputed dates of the earthquake and the fall of Ithome; for which see A. W. Gomme, *Commentary on Thucydides*, I, pp. 401–8.

ᵘ Arnold Toynbee first detected Thucydides' error in *JHS* XXXIII (1913), pp. 262–72; it is curious that Xenophon should by another error get the same total. On the organization of the army of the *morae* see H. T. Wade-Gery, *Essays in Greek History*, pp. 71–7, 80–5, and G. E. Underhill, *Commentary on the Hellenica of Xenophon*, pp. 347–9. After Leuctra there were only twelve *lochoi* (Xen. *Hell.* VII. iv. 20; v. 10), but this was probably due to a reorganization of the army in which the *mora* (not mentioned after Leuctra) was abolished.

ᵛ Attested cases where the Spartans intervened in other cities in the oligarchic interest are Athens (Herod. V. 69–70), Megara (Thuc. IV. 74), Sicyon (Thuc. V. 81), Argos (Thuc. V. 76, 81–3), Elis (Xen. *Hell.* III. ii. 27 ff.), Corinth (Xen. *Hell.* V. i. 34), Mantinea (Xen. *Hell.* V. ii. 7), Phlius (Xen. *Hell.* V. ii. 8–10, iii. 25). Attested cases of Athens installing democracies are Erythrae (Tod, *Greek Hist. Inscr.* 29), Colophon (*SEG.* X. 17) and Samos (Thuc. I. 115). On the ideological conflict see Thuc. III. 82 ff.

ʷ On the development of the office of harmost see H. W. Parke in *JHS* L (1930), pp. 37 ff. and LII (1932), pp. 44 ff.

ˣ See G. T. Griffith, 'The Union of Corinth and Argos (392–386 B.C.)', *Historia*, I (1950), 236–56.

ʸ Pausanias (VIII. xxvii. 11) wrongly makes the defeated king Acrotatus, son of Cleomenes.

ᶻ Pausanias (VIII. x. 8, VIII. xxxvii. 13) by a natural mistake substitutes King Agis IV, son of King Eudamidas II, for Agis, son of Eudamidas in the collateral line.

ᵃᵃ On the much disputed date of the battle of Sellasia, see F. W. Walbank, *A Historical Commentary on Polybius*, I. 272.

ᵇᵇ The account of the origin of the ephorate in Plut. *Cleom.* 10 has a certain plausibility. The title ('overseer') is more appropriate to royal delegates than to champions of the people, and some of the functions of the ephors, especially their general disciplinary powers and their jurisdiction in civil suits, are more easily explained if they had originally been royal officers. In that case I would postulate that the people insisted on electing the ephors themselves.

^{cc} It is interesting that Pericleidas, the Spartan envoy in 461 (Aristoph. *Lysistrata*, 1138, Plut. *Cimon*, 16), called his son Athenaeus, and that Athenaeus was one of the three Spartans who swore to the truce in 423 and was sent to Chalcidice to make Brasidas observe it (Thuc. IV. 119, 122). Athenaeus might have been a contemporary of Cimon's son Lacedaemonius (Plut. *Cimon*, 16). One may infer that Pericleidas and his son were both of the party which favoured the dual hegemony policy, and that perhaps Pericleidas was a friend of Cimon, who upheld this policy.

INDEX OF SOURCES

LITERARY AUTHORITIES

176

INSCRIPTIONS, COINS AND PAPYRI

GENERAL INDEX

Abydos, 86, 108, 113–14; battle, 89
Acanthus, 119, 121
Acarnania, 106–7, 113, 125, 132
Achaea, 65, 72, 113, 125, 127, 129, 139–40, 143–5, 150–1, 153–5, 157–8, 161–4
Acoris, king of Egypt, 127
Acragas, 151
Acrotatus, king, 151
Acrotatus, son of Cleomenes II, 148, 151
Aegina, 51, 53–5, 61, 63–5, 67, 113–15
Aegospotami, battle, 92
Aegys, 11, 131
Aeneas of Stymphalus, 141
Aenianes, 71, 104, 107
Aeschines of Sicyon, 45–6, 173
Aethaea, 8, 61
Aetolia, 113, 150, 157–8, 161
Agasicles, king, 1, 3, 5
agathoergos (Benefactor), 32, 44
Agesilaus (Agis), grandfather of Leotychidas, 3
Agesilaus, king, 27, 36, 39, 62, 98, 100–1, 106–8, 110–13, 116, 118, 120–6, 128–130, 132, 134, 145–8
Agesilaus, ephor, 21, 23, 153
Agesilaus, son of Eudamidas, 157
Agesipolis I, king, 107, 115, 118, 121, 147–8
Agesipolis II, king, 148
Agesipolis III, king, 157–8
Agesipolis, son of Cleombrotus II, 157
Agiads, 23; *see* family tree after p. 189
Agiatis, 154
Agis I, king, 11
Agis II, king, 15, 39, 74, 78–81, 83–4, 86, 92, 97–8, 157
Agis III, king, 149–50
Agis IV, king, 21, 23–4, 40, 152–4
Agis, son of Eudamidas, 151
Agis (Agesilaus), *see* Agesilaus (Agis)
agoranomi, 166
Alabanda, 11
Alcetas, Spartan, 125–6
Alcibiades, 78, 81–2, 84–7, 89–90, 92, 98
Alcidas, navarch, 37, 71
Alcman, 3, 38
Alexamenus, Aetolian, 161
Alexander the Great, 150
Amasis, king of Egypt, 46–7
Amblada, 11

Ambracia, 45–6, 106, 127
Amorges, Persian, 83
Amphipolis, 73, 75–6
Amyclae, 11, 32, 38, 61, 112
Amyntas, king of Macedon, 119–20
Anaxandridas, son of Theopompus, king (?), 3
Anaxandridas, king, 1, 18, 27, 45, 48
Anaxibius, Spartan, 113
Anaxidamus, king (?), 3
Anaxilaus, king (?), 3
Anchimolius, navarch, 50
Andocides, 110
Androcleides, Theban, 103–4
Angelus, Thessalian, 46
Antalcidas, navarch, 110–11, 114–15
Antalcidas, Peace of, *see* King's Peace
Antigonus, Monophthalmus, 149
Antigonus, Gonatas, 151
Antigonus, Doson, 155–6
Antiochus, Athenian, 90
Antiochus, Arcadian, 140–1
Antipater, regent of Macedonia, 150
Antissa, 113
Antisthenes, Spartan, 85
Antitheus, Theban, 103
Antony, 165
Apollonia, 119, 121
Apollodorus, Athenian, 4
Appius Claudius, 164
Aracus, navarch, 91
Aratus of Sicyon, 151, 153–5
Arcadia, 53, 60, 78–80, 83, 109, 125, 130–132, 138–45, 150
Archestratus, Athenian, 93
Archidamus I, king, 21, 27, 39, 63, 65, 67–68, 71, 74, 118
Archidamus II, king, 123, 129, 133, 139, 143–4, 148–9
Archidamus III, king, 150
Archidamus V, king, 154, 157
Archidamus, son of Theopompus, 3
Archidamus, king (?), 3
Archilaus, king, 11
Areus I, king, 39, 150–1
Argeia, 13
Arginusae, battle, 91
Argos, 46, 53, 56, 60, 63, 65, 74, 76–81, 85, 102–3, 106–11, 115, 118, 132, 138–9, 142, 144–5, 149–50, 155, 157, 159–60

184

Arimas, *lochos*, 32
Ariobarzanes, 115, 139
Aristagoras, Milesian, 51–2
Aristodemus, king, 13
Aristodemus, regent, 107
Aristodemus, Megalopolitan, 151
Aristogenes, Milesian, 46
Aristomedes, Thessalian, 46
Ariston, king, 1, 3, 45, 54
Aristotle, views on early Sparta, 4, 6, 31, 41–2
Armenas, son of Nabis, 162
army, 32–3, 61–3, 174
art, 38
Artaxerxes II, 96, 101, 115, 127
Artemis Orthia, 35, 166
Asea, 145
Asine, 8, 133, 139
Aspendus, 87, 112
assembly, 15, 18, 21–5, 27, 59–60, 67, 97–8, 113, 118, 128, 152–3; little assembly, 99
Asteropus, ephor, 29
Astias, Theban, 103
Astyochus, navarch, 85, 87
Athenaeus, Spartan, 175
Athens, 49–57, 59–61, 63–96, 102–16, 118, 122–30, 132, 134, 138, 150, 142, 144–146, 151
Augustus, 165
Aules, Phocian, 46

Benefactor, *see agathoergos*
bideoi, 166
Boeotia, 63–4, 72, 75, 77–80, 82–3, 93, 95, 97, 100, 103–7, 110–13, 118, 126, 128, 132, 145; *see also* Thebes
Brasidas, 37, 73
Byzantium, 57–8, 87, 90, 112, 125

Caecilius Metellus, 163
Callibius, Spartan, 94
Callibius, Tegeate, 130–1
Callicratidas, navarch, 37, 90–1
Calydon, 113, 140
Caphyae, 151, 154
Cardamyle, 165
Carneia, 33, 166
Carthage, 20, 148
Cassander, 150
Caunus, 85, 101
cavalry, 32, 63
Cephallenia, 127
Chabrias, Athenian, 123, 126, 138
Chalcedon, 90, 112
Chares, Athenian, 141–2

Chalcideus, Spartan, 84
Chalcidice, 73, 75–6, 106
Charilaus, king, 4, 6
Chilon, ephor, 45, 173
Chilon, pretender, 157
Chios, 57, 84, 108, 125
Cibyra, 11
Cimon, 61
Cinadon, Spartan, 18, 27, 99
Cinurians, 131
Clazomenae, 84, 116
Cleandridas, father of Gylippus, 38, 65, 81
Cleandridas, Spartan, 126
Clearidas, Spartan, 76
Cleisthenes, Athenian, 50
Cleitor, 124
Cleombrotus I, king, 122–4, 126, 128
Cleombrotus II, king, 153, 157
Cleombrotus, regent, 1, 48, 57, 63
Cleomenes I, king, 1, 15, 48–55
Cleomenes II, king, 148
Cleomenes III, king, 29, 154–7
Cleon, Athenian, 72–3
Cleonymus, son of Cleomenes II, 148–9, 151–2
Cleophon, Athenian, 89, 91
Cnemus, navarch, 37
Cnidus, 85, 111; battle, 107
Coeratadas, Theban, 103
Common Peace, 147; *see also* King's Peace
Conon, Athenian, 91–2, 100–1, 107–8, 110
Conoura, obe, 32
Corinth, 45–7, 51, 63, 66–7, 75–6, 79–83, 93, 95, 97, 102, 104, 106–12, 115, 118, 125, 127, 129, 133, 138, 141–3, 155; League of, 150
Corcyra, 66–7, 126–7
Coronea, battle, 107
Cos, 108
Cratesippidas, navarch, 89–90
Crete, 11, 20, 34, 41, 107, 151, 159–60
Critias, Athenian, 26, 95
Crius, Aeginetan, 54
Croesus, 46–7
Cromnus, 144
Croton, 11
Cynuria, 11, 46, 77, 81; *see also* Thyreatis
Cynossema, battle, 88
Cyprus, 57, 92, 100, 116
Cypselids, 45–6
Cyrene, 29
Cyrus, king of Persia, 46
Cyrus, son of Darius II, 90–1, 96
Cythera, 8, 46, 72, 74–5, 108, 165
Cyzicus, battle, 90

185

186

187

oligarchy, supported by Sparta, 50, 70, 81, 94–5, 97, 118–22, 174
Olympia, 6, 78, 97, 115, 143–4
Olynthus, 119–21
Orchomenus (Arcadia), 79, 124, 132–3, 151
Orchomenus (Boeotia), 105, 107, 110, 114, 124
Orestes, bones, 44

paedonomus, 35, 166
Pallantium, 145
Panactum, 75, 78
Parrhasians, 77, 131, 139
Partheniae, 12
Patrae, 78
patronomi, 154, 165
Pausanias, regent, 57–9, 63
Pausanias, king, 27, 92, 95–6, 105–6, 118
Peace of Antalcidas, *see* King's Peace
Peace of Callias, 64, 83, 117
peers, 36
Pegae, 65, 72
Peisander, navarch, 107
Pellene, 79, 83, 107, 133, 138, 141, 155
Pelopidas, 124, 140
Peloponnesian League, 44–5, 51–2, 66–7, 70, 80–1, 93, 113, 119, 121, 124–6, 143
Pelops, king, 158
peltasts, 109, 112–13, 127, 132
pentecoster, pentecostys, 62
Perdiccas, king of Macedon, 73
Pericleidas, Spartan, 175
Pericles, 64–5, 70–1
Perinthus, 90
Perioeci, 8–9, 14, 29, 40, 61, 72, 99, 120–1, 130, 132–4, 153–4, 159–60, 162, 165
Persia, 46, 49–53, 55–8, 64, 83–91, 96–7, 99–103, 106, 108, 110–11, 114–17, 127, 139–41, 149–50
Pharacides, Spartan, 115
Pharae, 165
Pharax, navarch, 101
Pharis, 11
Pharnabazus, 83–6, 89, 96, 98, 100–1, 107–8
pheiditia, 36–7, 153, 165
Phigaleia, 151
Phillidas, Theban, 122
Philip II of Macedon, 149–50
Philip V of Macedon, 158–9
Philiscus of Abydos, 139
Philomelus, Phocian, 149
Philopoemen, 158, 161–3
Phlius, 79, 109, 118, 121, 125, 129, 133, 138, 141, 143, 155

Phocis, 46, 63–4, 80, 83, 104, 107, 125–8, 132, 149
Phoebidas, Spartan, 120, 124
phratries, 23
Pitane, obe, Pitanates, *lochos*, 32
Plataea, 49, 52, 60–1, 70, 75, 118, 122–3, 128; battle, 57
Pleistarchus, king, 57
Pleistoanax, king, 63, 65, 73–4, 77
Ploas, *lochos*, 32
polemarchs, 61–2, 109
Polemarchus, Spartan, 32
Pollis, navarch, 126
Polybiades, Spartan, 121
Polycrates of Samos, 47, 49
Polydamas of Pherae, 126
Polydorus, king, 2, 4, 31–2, 40
population, 10, 62, 129–30, 134–6, 152
Potidaea, 66–7, 71, 120–1
Prasiae, 81, 133
Praxitas, Spartan, 109
Prothous, Spartan, 21, 128
Proxenus, Tegeate, 130–1
Prytanis, king, 6
Ptolemy II, 151
Pylos, 61, 72, 74, 77
Pyrrhus, king of Epirus, 151
Pythagoras, Spartan, 159
Pythii, 14

rhetra of 'Lycurgus', 7, 17–18, 24, 26, 28, 31, 172; enactments of the assembly, 17–18, 22–4, 42, 136, 152–3
Rhianus, 3
Rhodes, 85, 89, 101, 111–12, 125
Rome, 158–65

Sacred War, 149
Sagalassus, 11
Salaethus, Spartan, 71
Samius, navarch, 96
Samos, 47, 49–50, 57, 66, 84–5, 87, 92, 111
Sciritae, 8, 61, 80, 120, 133
Scyros, 110, 116
Scythians, 50
Selge, 11
Sellasia, battle, 155–6
Selymbria, 90
Sepeia, battle, 53
Sestos, 57, 86, 88, 108
Sicily, 71, 82–3, 85–8
Sicyon, 79, 81–3, 107–9, 125, 129, 138, 140–2, 149, 151
Simonides on Lycurgus, 6
Sinis, *lochos*, 32
Sosibius the Laconian, 4, 33
Sous, king, 11

188

These genealogies are based on Pausanias III. ii–x; Eus. *Chron.* I. 222 ff.;
Herodotus VII. 204, VIII. 131, IX. 10; Plut. *Lyc.* 1–2, *Agis* 1; Diodorus
XI. 45, 48, XII. 35, XIII. 65, XIV. 89, XV. 23, 60, 93, XVI. 63, XVII.
63, XX. 29; Thuc. I. 107, 114, III. 26, V. 16; Xen. *Hell.* III. i. 6, iii. 1–4,
IV. ii. 9, V. iii. 18, *Anab.* II. i. 3, VII. viii. 17; Polyb. IV. 35, X. 41, XI. 17,
XIII. 6, XVI. 3, XX. 13; Diod. XXVIII. 1; Livy XXXIV. 32, XXXV.
35–6; *Syll*[3]. 381, 584. The pedigrees are fully discussed by P. Poralla,
Prosopographie der Lakedaimonier, pp. 137–72.

[1] Sous is omitted in Herod. VIII. 131.
[2] Simonides made Lycurgus the son of Prytanis, and presumably brother
of Polydectes, omitting Eunomus (Plut. *Lyc.* 2).
[3] Known only from Barbarus Scaligeri. In the text of Eusebius 30 years
are missing, and either that has to be added to Agis' one year, or
Menelaus must be accepted with 30.
[4] This and the next four names are the version of Pausanias III. vii.
[5] This and the next four names are the version of Herod. VIII. 131.

Ordinary letters denote kings.
Small capitals denote regents.
Italics denote members of royal families.

Cleomene
(c. 520–

Gorgo
(=Leonid

—(398–61)
Agesipolis I I (361–38)

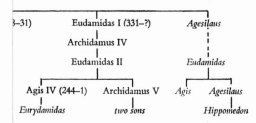